KV-511-139

CAKES & BAKES

LAKELAND

Lakeland and Bauer Media Ltd hereby exclude all liability to the extent permitted by law for any errors or omission in this book and for any loss, damage or expense (whether direct or indirect) suffered by a third party relying on any information contained in this book.

This book was created in 2014 for Lakeland by AWW Books, an imprint of Octopus Publishing Group Ltd, based on materials licensed to it by Bauer Media Books, Sydney.

Bauer Media Limited
54 Park St, Sydney
GPO Box 4088, Sydney, NSW 2001
www.awwcookbooks.com.au

BAUER
MEDIA GROUP

OCTOPUS PUBLISHING GROUP
Design – Chris Bell
Food Director – Pamela Clark

Published for Lakeland in the United Kingdom by Octopus Publishing Group Limited

Endeavour House
189 Shaftesbury Avenue
London WC2H 8JY
United Kingdom
phone + 44 (0) 207 632 5400;
fax + 44 (0) 207 632 5405
aww@octopusbooks.co.uk;
www.octopusbooks.co.uk
www.australian-womens-weekly.com

Printed and bound in China

A catalogue record for this book is available from the British Library.

ISBN 978-1-909770-15-7

© Bauer Media Limited 2014
ABN 18 053 273 546
This publication is copyright. No part of it may be reproduced or transmitted in any form without the written permission of the Publisher.

The Department of Health advises that eggs should not be consumed raw. This book contains some cakes made with lightly cooked eggs. It is prudent for vulnerable people such as pregnant and nursing mothers, invalids, the elderly, babies and young children to avoid lightly cooked eggs. Recipes using lightly cooked eggs should be refrigerated and used promptly.

This book also includes dishes made with nuts and nut derivatives. It is advisable for those with known allergic reactions to nuts and nut derivatives and those who may be potentially vulnerable to these allergies, such as pregnant and nursing mothers, invalids, the elderly, babies and children to avoid dishes made with nuts and nut oils. It is also prudent to check the labels of pre-prepared ingredients for the possible inclusion of nut derivatives.

Some of the recipes in this book have appeared in other publications.

CAKES & BAKES

60 DELICIOUS RECIPES FOR EVERY OCCASION

Illustrated with beautiful colour photographs, this is an irresistible collection of 60 cakes and bakes, from easy traybakes and tempting miniature creations to showstopping party cakes and festive treats. You'll find something to share with family and friends, whatever the occasion.

With every recipe triple-tested® for perfect results, this excellent cookbook is sure to be one of the best loved on your kitchen bookshelf. To discover the rest of our range of cookbooks, together with our unrivalled selection of creative kitchenware, visit one of our friendly Lakeland stores or shop online at www.lakeland.co.uk.

CONTENTS

BAKING BASICS

Getting the best from your oven

There are so many types and makes of oven, so it's important that you get to know yours, particularly when it comes to baking. A reliable oven is essential for success and it is a good idea to check the thermostat for accuracy with an oven thermometer.

If you are using a fan-assisted oven, check the operating instructions for best results. As a general rule, position the oven racks and tin so that the top of the cooked cake will be roughly in the centre of the oven. Always bake in an oven preheated to the correct temperature – this usually takes at least 10 minutes.

Preparing cake tins

Each recipe will indicate whether the tin needs to be greased or greased and lined.

To line a cake tin, trace around the base with a pencil onto baking parchment. Cut out the shape slightly inside the pencil line, so that the paper fits snugly inside the tin. If you need to line the sides of the tin, make a baking parchment 'collar', extending it about 5cm above the top of the tin. Cut a parchment strip long enough to fit around the inside of the tin and 8cm wider than its depth. Fold the strip lengthways about 2cm from the edge and make short, diagonal cuts about 2cm apart, up to the fold. This helps ease the paper around the curve, with the cut section fitting around the base of the tin.

Position the circle of parchment over the base of the tin after lining the sides.

Is it done?

All baking times are approximate. Check just after the suggested time – the cake should be brown and starting to shrink away from the sides of the tin. The top should feel firm to your fingertips.

To grease a cake tin, use either a light, even coating of cooking oil spray or use a pastry brush to brush melted butter evenly over the base and sides of the tin. Whether using aluminium, non-stick or silicone tins, ensure the surface is unscratched.

To test if a cake is cooked, insert a thin metal skewer into the deepest part of the cake from top to base. As the skewer is removed gently, it should have no uncooked mixture clinging to it. Do not confuse mixture with stickiness from fruit.

Cooling cakes and bakes

We have indicated where is it best to leave something to cool completely in the tin. Generally, we suggest leaving cakes in their tins for up to 15 minutes to cool before turning out onto a wire rack to cool completely.

Wire racks can mark a soft cake, such as a sponge. To prevent this, cover the rack with baking parchment.

What went wrong?

The cake sinks in the middle when removed from the oven Generally this means the cake is undercooked.

The cake sinks in the middle while still baking This indicates the oven is too hot.

The cake has a sugary crust The butter and cream have not been creamed sufficiently.

The cake has white specks on top This indicates undissolved sugar or insufficient creaming.

The cake rises and cracks in the centre The cake tin is too small or the oven is too hot (NB: most cakes baked in loaf tins crack slightly).

The cake shrinks excessively The oven was too hot and has caused the cake to overcook.

The cake sticks to the tin There was too much sugar or other sweetening in the recipe. If a recipe contains honey or syrup, or if the cake tin is new, grease the tin and line with greased baking parchment.

The cake is crusty, overbrowned and uncooked in centre This means the cake was baked too long or at too high a temperature or that the cake tin was too small, causing top to overcook.

The cake crumbles when it is cut The mixture may have been creamed too much or the eggs added too quickly.

The cake is pale on top with a brown bottom and sides The tin was too large or the lining paper was too high above the tin.

The cake rises unevenly The oven shelf was not straight, the oven was not level or the mixture was not spread evenly in the tin.

The fruit sinks to the bottom The fruit has not been dried thoroughly or the cake mixture was too soft to support the fruit.

> **TOP TIPS**
> • Always have ingredients, especially eggs and butter, at room temperature.
> • When measuring liquids, always stand the measuring jug on a flat surface and check at eye level for accuracy.
> • Level off spoon measurements with a knife or spatula.
> • An electric mixer is not essential, but it certainly makes the process easier and faster.
> • Always be guided by the recipe and use the type of flour and sugar specified.
> • It is best to use the shape and size of tin the recipe suggests because, for example, the volume of a deep 20cm round tin is not the same as a deep 20cm square tin.

To turn out a cake, hold the tin firmly and shake it gently; this helps loosen the cake. Turn the cake upside-down onto a wire rack, then turn the cake topside-up immediately, using a second rack. When turning soft cakes, cover the racks with baking parchment.

To split a cake into even layers, use skewers as a guide for the knife. For large cakes, push long skewers through the cake; for small cakes, use toothpicks to mark the layer. Use a sharp serrated knife to split the cake. Cut the cake barely above the skewers.

To melt chocolate, place roughly chopped chocolate into a heatproof bowl over a pan of barely simmering water. The water mustn't touch the base of the bowl. Stir the chocolate until smooth, and remove from the pan as soon as it's melted.

CLASSIC
CAKES & BAKES

ICED GINGERBREAD

125g butter, softened
110g dark brown sugar
2 eggs
250g plain flour
½ teaspoon bicarbonate of soda
2 teaspoons ground ginger
360g treacle
2 tablespoons milk
55g finely chopped glacé ginger
55g finely chopped raisins

lemon glacé icing
160g icing sugar
10g butter, softened
1 tablespoon lemon juice
1 tablespoon boiling water,
   approximately

1 Preheat oven to 180°C/160°C fan-assisted. Grease 20cm x 30cm rectangular cake tin; line base and sides with baking parchment, extending the paper 5cm above sides.
2 Beat butter and sugar in a small bowl with an electric mixer until light and fluffy. Beat in eggs, one at a time. Transfer mixture to a large bowl; stir in sifted flour, bicarbonate of soda and ground ginger, treacle, milk, glacé ginger and raisins. Spread mixture into tin.
3 Bake cake about 45 minutes. Stand in tin 5 minutes; turn, top-side up, onto a wire rack to cool.
4 Meanwhile, make lemon glacé icing.
5 Spread cake with icing. Stand until icing is set before cutting.

lemon glacé icing
Sift icing sugar into a medium bowl. Stir in butter, juice and enough of the water until icing is smooth and spreadable.

prep + cook time 1 hour
makes 16
tips Iced cake will keep in an airtight container for up to 3 days. Uniced cake can be frozen for up to 3 months.
• Serve warm as a dessert with cream or custard.

ORANGE CAKE

150g butter, softened
1 tablespoon finely grated
   orange rind
150g caster sugar
3 eggs
225g self-raising flour
60ml milk

orange icing
120g icing sugar
1½ tablespoons orange juice

1 Preheat oven to 180°C/160°C fan-assisted. Grease deep 20cm round cake tin.

2 Beat butter, rind, sugar, eggs, flour and milk in medium bowl with electric mixer at low speed until just combined. Increase speed to medium, beat about 3 minutes or until mixture is smooth.

3 Spread mixture into tin; bake about 40 minutes. Stand cake in tin 5 minutes; turn, top-side up, onto wire rack to cool.

4 Make orange icing. Spread icing over top of cake.

orange icing
Stir ingredients in small bowl until smooth.

prep + cook time 50 minutes
serves 12

WHISKY FRUIT CAKE

300g raisins
150g dried apricots
150g red glacé cherries
240g sultanas
160g currants
180ml water
125ml whisky
250g butter
220g light brown sugar
½ teaspoon bicarbonate of soda
4 eggs
185g self-raising flour
185g plain flour
60g pecans
55g blanched almonds
45g roasted pistachios
2 tablespoons whisky, extra

1 Preheat oven to 150°C/130°C fan-assisted. Grease deep 22cm round cake tin; line base and side with two thicknesses of baking parchment, extending paper 5cm above edge.

2 Coarsely chop raisins, apricots and cherries. Transfer to a large saucepan with sultanas, currants, the water, whisky, chopped butter, sugar and bicarbonate of soda; stir over medium heat until butter is melted and sugar dissolved. Bring to the boil; remove from heat. Transfer to a large bowl; cool to room temperature. Stir lightly beaten eggs into fruit mixture, then stir in sifted flours.

3 Spread mixture evenly into tin. Tap on worktop; level top. Scatter with combined nuts, pressing in slightly. Bake cake about 2 hours 40 minutes.

4 Brush hot cake with extra whisky. Cover hot cake with foil; cool cake in tin overnight.

prep + cook time 3 hours 15 minutes (+ cooling time)
serves 36
tip Cake can be made up to 6 months ahead; store in an airtight container in the refrigerator, or freeze for up to 12 months.

MADEIRA CAKE

180g butter, softened
2 teaspoons finely grated lemon
 rind
150g caster sugar
3 eggs
110g plain flour
110g self-raising flour
55g mixed peel
35g chopped almonds

1 Preheat oven to 160°C/140°C fan-assisted. Grease deep 20cm round cake tin; line base with baking parchment.

2 Beat butter, rind and sugar in small bowl with electric mixer until light and fluffy. Beat in eggs, one at a time. Transfer mixture to large bowl; stir in sifted flours.

3 Spread mixture into tin; bake 20 minutes. Remove cake from oven; sprinkle with peel and nuts. Return to oven; bake about 40 minutes. Stand cake in tin 5 minutes; turn, top-side up, onto wire rack to cool.

prep + cook time 1 hour 15 minutes
serves 12

SWISS ROLL

3 eggs, separated
110g caster sugar
2 tablespoons hot milk
110g self-raising flour
55g caster sugar, extra
160g raspberry jam, warmed

1 Preheat oven to 200°C/180°C fan-assisted. Grease a 23cm x 32cm swiss roll tin; line base and long sides with baking parchment, extending the paper 5cm over sides.

2 Beat egg whites in a small bowl with an electric mixer until soft peaks form; gradually add sugar, beating until sugar dissolves. With motor operating, add egg yolks, one at a time, beating until mixture is pale and thick; this will take about 10 minutes.

3 Working quickly, pour hot milk down side of bowl; add triple-sifted flour and gently fold milk and flour through egg mixture (see tip). Spread mixture into tin.

4 Bake sponge about 8 minutes.

5 Meanwhile, place a piece of baking parchment cut the same size as the swiss roll tin on worktop; sprinkle evenly with extra sugar.

6 Turn cake immediately onto the sugared paper; peel away lining paper. Use a serrated knife to trim edges from all sides of cake. Using paper as a guide, gently roll warm cake loosely from one of the short sides. Unroll; cool. Spread evenly with jam. Reroll cake from same short side.

prep + cook time 30 minutes
serves 10
tips Gently fold the milk and flour into the egg mixture, taking care to keep as much air in the mixture as possible. Heavy mixing will reduce the amount of air incorporated in the mixture and will cause the sponge to be flat and heavy.
• Swiss roll is best eaten the day it is made.

TRIPLE CHOCOLATE BROWNIES

125g butter, chopped
200g dark eating chocolate, chopped
110g caster sugar
2 eggs
185g plain flour
150g white eating chocolate, chopped
100g milk eating chocolate, chopped

1 Preheat oven to 180°C/160°C fan-assisted. Grease deep 19cm square cake tin; line base with baking parchment, extending paper 5cm over sides.

2 Stir butter and dark chocolate in medium saucepan over low heat until smooth. Let cool 10 minutes.

3 Stir in sugar and eggs then sifted flour and white and milk chocolates. Spread mixture into tin.

4 Bake brownies about 35 minutes. Cool in tin before cutting into 16 squares.

prep + cook time 1 hour
makes 16

VICTORIA SPONGE

250g butter
1 teaspoon vanilla extract
220g caster sugar
4 eggs
80ml milk
300g self-raising flour
110g raspberry jam, warmed
1 tablespoon icing sugar, for
  dusting

1 Preheat oven to 180°C/160°C fan-assisted. Grease two deep 20cm round cake tins; line bases with baking parchment.
2 Beat butter, extract and sugar in small bowl with electric mixer until light and fluffy. Beat in eggs, one at a time. Add milk and beat well. Transfer mixture to large bowl. Stir in half the sifted flour, then remaining sifted flour; stir until the mixture is smooth.
3 Divide mixture between tins; bake about 30 minutes.
4 Turn cakes onto baking-parchment-covered wire rack to cool. Sandwich cakes with jam; dust with a little sifted icing sugar.

prep + cook time 50 minutes
serves 10

MARBLE CAKE

250g butter, softened
1 teaspoon vanilla extract
275g caster sugar
3 eggs
335g self-raising flour
180ml milk
pink food colouring
2 tablespoons cocoa powder
2 tablespoons milk, extra

butter frosting
125g butter, softened
320g icing sugar
2 tablespoons milk

1 Preheat oven to 180°C/160°C fan-assisted. Grease a deep 22cm round cake tin; line base with baking parchment.
2 Beat butter, extract and sugar in a medium bowl with an electric mixer until light and fluffy. Beat in eggs, one at a time. Stir in sifted flour and milk, in two batches.
3 Divide mixture into three bowls; tint one mixture pink. Blend sifted cocoa with extra milk in a cup; stir into second mixture. Leave remaining mixture plain. Drop alternate spoonfuls of mixtures into tin. Pull a skewer backwards and forwards through cake mixture to create a marble effect.
4 Bake cake about 1 hour. Stand in tin 5 minutes; turn, top-side up, onto a wire rack to cool.
5 Meanwhile, make butter frosting.
6 Spread frosting all over cake.

butter frosting
Beat butter in a small bowl with an electric mixer until light and fluffy; beat in sifted icing sugar and milk, in two batches.

prep + cook time 1 hour 40 minutes
serves 12
tips The traditional colours for a marble cake are chocolate brown, pink and white, but you can use any food colouring you like. Make the colours fairly strong for maximum impact, as they may fade during baking.
• Cake will keep in an airtight container, at room temperature, for up to 3 days. Uniced cake can be frozen for up to 3 months.

CARROT CAKE

3 eggs
250g light brown sugar
250ml vegetable oil
540g coarsely grated carrot
120g coarsely chopped walnuts
375g self-raising flour
½ teaspoon bicarbonate of soda
2 teaspoons mixed spice

lemon cream cheese frosting
45g butter, softened
110g cream cheese, softened
1½ teaspoons finely grated
   lemon rind
360g icing sugar

1 Preheat oven to 180°C/160°C fan-assisted. Grease a deep 22cm round cake tin; line the base with baking parchment.
2 Beat eggs, sugar and oil in a small bowl with an electric mixer until thick and creamy. Transfer mixture to a large bowl; stir in carrot and nuts, then sifted dry ingredients. Pour mixture into tin.
3 Bake cake about 1 hour 15 minutes. Stand in tin 5 minutes; turn, top-side up, onto a wire rack to cool.
4 Meanwhile, make lemon cream cheese frosting.
5 Split cake in half, place bottom layer onto a serving plate, cut-side up; spread with half the frosting. Top with remaining cake layer; spread top with remaining frosting.

lemon cream cheese frosting
Beat butter, cream cheese and rind in a small bowl with an electric mixer until light and fluffy; gradually beat in sifted icing sugar.

prep + cook time 1 hour 25 minutes
serves 12
tips You need three large carrots for the amount of grated carrot used in this recipe.
• Cake will keep in an airtight container in the refrigerator for up to 3 days. Without the frosting, cake can be frozen for up to 3 months.

TRADITIONAL SCONES

375g self-raising flour
1 tablespoon caster sugar
¼ teaspoon salt
30g butter
180ml milk
125ml water, approximately

1 Preheat oven to 220°C/200°C fan-assisted. Grease deep 19cm square cake tin.
2 Sift flour, sugar and salt into large bowl; rub in butter with fingertips. Make well in centre of mixture; add milk and almost all of the water. Using a knife, cut the milk and the water through the flour mixture to mix to a soft, sticky dough. Add remaining water only if needed. Knead dough on floured surface until smooth.
3 Press dough out evenly to 2cm thickness. Cut as many 4.5cm rounds as you can from dough. Place rounds side by side, just touching, in tin. Gently knead scraps of dough together; repeat pressing and cutting of dough, place in same tin. Brush tops with a little extra milk.
4 Bake scones about 15 minutes or until browned and scones sound hollow when tapped firmly on the top with fingers.

prep + cook time 45 minutes
makes 16
tip For date scones, when making the basic scone mixture, stir 120g finely chopped pitted dried dates into the flour mixture after the butter has been rubbed in and replace the milk and water with 310ml buttermilk.

FAMILY CAKES & BAKES

GINGER & PEAR MUFFINS

300g self-raising flour
1 teaspoon ground ginger
165g caster sugar
80g butter, melted
280g natural yogurt
2 eggs
2 medium pears (460g), peeled,
  chopped finely

muesli topping
50g butter
2 tablespoons honey
220g unsweetened muesli

1 Preheat oven to 200°C/180°C fan-assisted. Line 12-hole (80ml) muffin pan with paper cases.
2 Make muesli topping.
3 Sift flour and ginger into large bowl; stir in sugar and combined butter, yogurt and eggs. Do not overmix; mixture should be lumpy. Gently stir in pears.
4 Spoon mixture into pan holes; spoon muesli topping onto muffin mixture. Bake about 20 minutes. Stand muffins in pan 5 minutes; turn, top-side up, onto wire rack to cool.

muesli topping
Stir butter and honey in small saucepan over low heat until combined. Remove from heat; stir in muesli.

prep + cook time 35 minutes
makes 12

APRICOT & HONEY ROCK CAKES

160g wholemeal self-raising flour
150g white self-raising flour
55g caster sugar
¼ teaspoon ground cinnamon
90g butter, chopped
80g finely chopped dried apricots
2 tablespoons sultanas
1 egg
2 tablespoons honey
80ml milk

1 Preheat oven to 200°C/180°C fan-assisted. Grease two oven trays.
2 Sift dry ingredients into large bowl; rub in butter. Stir in apricots and sultanas. Combine egg and honey in small bowl; stir into mixture with milk.
3 Drop tablespoonfuls of the mixture in rough heaps onto trays. Bake rock cakes, uncovered, about 15 minutes. Cool on trays.

prep + cook time 35 minutes
makes 15
tips Try 2 tablespoons orange marmalade as an alternative to honey and 100g quartered glacé cherries instead of apricots.
• Rock cakes are cooked when they still feel soft in the oven. When they look firm, push one with your finger. If it moves easily on the tray, the cakes are cooked; they will become firmer on cooling.
• Rock cakes can be stored in an airtight container for up to 2 days.

WHOLEMEAL BANANA & PRUNE BREAD

240g wholemeal self-raising flour
1 teaspoon ground cinnamon
2 teaspoons finely grated lemon
  rind
100g butter, softened
165g dark brown sugar
2 eggs
3 large bananas, mashed
170g pitted prunes, chopped
  coarsely

1 Preheat oven to 180°C/160°C fan-assisted. Grease 14cm x 21cm loaf tin; line base and long sides with baking parchment, extending paper 2cm over sides.
2 Sift flour and cinnamon into large bowl; add rind, butter, sugar and eggs. Beat with electric mixer on low speed until ingredients are combined. Increase speed to medium; beat mixture until smooth. Stir in banana and prunes. Spread mixture into tin.
3 Bake bread about 1 hour. Stand bread in tin 5 minutes; turn, top-side up, onto wire rack to cool.

prep + cook time 1 hour 15 minutes
serves 10
tip Make sure that the bananas are over-ripe; if they are under-ripe, they won't mash easily and may cause the cake to be too heavy.

DATE & LEMON TRAYBAKE

250g plain flour
150g chilled butter, chopped
  coarsely
1 egg, beaten lightly
1 teaspoon vanilla extract
1 teaspoon finely grated lemon
  rind
165g caster sugar
60g desiccated coconut
40g coarsely chopped walnuts
15g shredded coconut

date filling
250g pitted dried dates,
  chopped coarsely
110g caster sugar
160ml water
80ml lemon juice

1 Make date filling.
2 Preheat oven to 180°C/160°C fan-assisted. Grease a 20cm x 30cm rectangular tin; line base and long sides with baking parchment, extending the paper 5cm over sides.
3 Sift flour into a large bowl; rub in butter. Stir in combined egg, extract and rind, then sugar, desiccated coconut and walnuts.
4 Press half the flour mixture firmly over base of tin. Spread filling over base. Add shredded coconut to remaining flour mixture then sprinkle over filling.
5 Bake about 35 minutes. Cool in tin before cutting into pieces.

date filling
Bring dates, sugar and the water to the boil in a medium saucepan. Reduce heat; simmer, stirring, about 3 minutes or until dates are pulpy. Stir in juice; cool.

prep + cook time 1 hour 10 minutes
makes 16
tips This will keep in an airtight container for up to 3 days.
• Shredded coconut is available at health food stores and online. If you can't find it, you can use the same quantity of raw coconut chips (also available at health food stores) or desiccated coconut instead.

APPLE CUSTARD CAKE

200g butter, softened
110g caster sugar
2 eggs
185g self-raising flour
40g custard powder
2 medium green-skinned apples
 (300g), peeled, cored, sliced
 thinly
1 tablespoon butter, melted
2 teaspoons caster sugar, extra
½ teaspoon ground cinnamon

custard
2 tablespoons custard powder
55g caster sugar
250ml milk
20g butter
2 teaspoons vanilla extract

1 Make custard.
2 Preheat oven to 180°C/160°C fan-assisted. Grease a deep 22cm round cake tin; line base with baking parchment.
3 Beat butter and sugar in a small bowl with an electric mixer until light and fluffy. Beat in eggs, one at a time. Stir in sifted flour and custard powder.
4 Spread half the mixture into the tin, top with custard. Top custard with spoonfuls of remaining cake mixture; gently spread with a spatula to completely cover custard. Arrange apples on top; brush with melted butter, then sprinkle with combined extra sugar and cinnamon.
5 Bake cake about 1 hour 15 minutes; cool in tin. Sprinkle with extra caster sugar, if you like.

custard
Combine custard powder and sugar in a small saucepan; gradually add milk, stirring over heat until mixture thickens slightly. Remove from heat; stir in butter and extract. Transfer to a small bowl, cover surface with cling film to prevent a skin forming; cool. Whisk until smooth just before using.

prep + cook time 2 hours
serves 8
tip Cake is best eaten the day it is made.

CHERRY CAKE WITH VANILLA SUGAR

200g butter, softened
150g light brown sugar
2 teaspoons vanilla extract
2 eggs
300g self-raising flour
160ml buttermilk
425g canned pitted black
   cherries in syrup, drained
30g butter, melted

vanilla sugar
1 vanilla pod
110g granulated sugar

1 Preheat oven to 180°C/160°C fan-assisted. Grease a deep 22cm round cake tin; line base and side with baking parchment.
2 Beat softened butter, sugar and extract in a small bowl with an electric mixer until light and fluffy. Beat in eggs, one at a time. Stir in sifted flour and buttermilk, in two batches. Spread mixture into tin; top with cherries.
3 Bake cake about 1 hour. Stand in tin 10 minutes; turn, top-side up, onto a wire rack.
4 Meanwhile, make vanilla sugar.
5 Brush warm cake with melted butter; sprinkle with reserved vanilla sugar. Serve warm.

vanilla sugar
Split vanilla pod in half lengthways; scrape seeds into blender or processor. Add sugar; process until fine. Reserve 2 tablespoons for this recipe; store unused sugar in an airtight container for another use.

prep + cook time 1 hour 20 minutes
serves 10
tip Cake is best eaten the day it is made.

SEMOLINA & YOGURT LEMON SYRUP CAKE

250g butter, softened
1 tablespoon finely grated lemon
 rind
220g caster sugar
3 eggs, separated
150g self-raising flour
160g semolina
280g natural yogurt

lemon syrup
220g caster sugar
80ml lemon juice

1 Preheat oven to 180°C/160°C fan-assisted. Butter a 20cm baba tin or a deep 20cm fluted cake ring well; sprinkle with a little flour, shake out excess.
2 Beat the butter, rind and sugar in a small bowl with an electric mixer until light and fluffy. Beat in egg yolks. Transfer mixture to a large bowl; stir in sifted flour, semolina and yogurt.
3 Beat egg whites in a small bowl with an electric mixer until soft peaks form; fold egg whites into cake mixture, in two batches. Spread mixture into tin.
4 Bake cake about 50 minutes.
5 Meanwhile, make lemon syrup.
6 Stand cake in tin 5 minutes; turn onto a wire rack set over an oven tray. Pierce cake all over with a skewer; pour hot lemon syrup over hot cake.

lemon syrup
Stir ingredients in a small saucepan over heat, without boiling, until sugar dissolves. Bring to the boil, without stirring; remove from heat.

prep + cook time 1 hour 10 minutes
serves 8
tip Cake with keep in an airtight container for up to 3 days.

PLUM & BLUEBERRY CRUMBLE CAKE

200g butter, softened
165g caster sugar
2 eggs
150g self-raising flour
150g plain flour
180ml milk
1kg canned whole plums, drained
60g fresh blueberries
2 teaspoons icing sugar

spiced crumble topping
75g plain flour
50g chilled butter, chopped coarsely
60g shredded coconut
55g light brown sugar
1 teaspoon mixed spice

1 Preheat oven to 180°C/160°C fan-assisted. Grease a deep 22cm springform cake tin; line base and side with baking parchment.
2 Make spiced crumble topping.
3 Beat butter and sugar in a medium bowl with an electric mixer until light and fluffy. Beat in eggs, one at a time. Transfer mixture to a large bowl; fold in sifted flours and milk, in two batches. Spread mixture into tin.
4 Halve plums; discard stones. Place plums and blueberries on cake mixture. Sprinkle crumble topping over fruit.
5 Bake cake about 1 hour 30 minutes (cover cake with foil if browning too quickly). Stand in tin 10 minutes; remove from tin, transfer to a wire rack to cool. Sprinkle with sifted icing sugar. Serve cake warm or at room temperature.

spiced crumble topping
Blend or process ingredients until combined.

prep + cook time 2 hours
serves 12
tips Cake will keep in an airtight container, refrigerated, for up to 3 days. Reheat slices in the microwave to serve warm.
• Shredded coconut is available at health food stores and online. If you can't find it, you can use the same quantity of raw coconut chips (also available at health food stores) or desiccated coconut instead.

MARMALADE, GINGER & ALMOND TRAYBAKE

90g unsalted butter, softened
110g caster sugar
1 egg
100g plain flour
50g self-raising flour
340g orange marmalade
60g finely chopped glacé ginger
1 egg, beaten lightly, extra
120g flaked almonds
60g ground almonds
1 tablespoon icing sugar

1 Preheat oven to 160°C/140°C fan-assisted. Grease a 20cm x 30cm rectangular tin; line base and long sides with baking parchment, extending the paper 5cm over sides.

2 Beat butter, caster sugar and egg in a small bowl with an electric mixer until light and fluffy. Stir in sifted flours. Spread mixture into tin. Combine marmalade and ginger in a small bowl; spread over mixture.

3 Combine extra egg, 80g of the flaked almonds and ground almonds in a medium bowl. Spread almond mixture over marmalade; sprinkle with remaining nuts.

4 Bake about 40 minutes. Cool in tin. Dust with sifted icing sugar before cutting.

prep + cook time 1 hour
makes 24
tip Cake will keep in an airtight container for up to a week.

INDULGENT
CAKES & BAKES

EGGNOG APPLE CAKE
WITH BROWN BUTTER FROSTING

4 small green apples (520g),
    peeled, chopped finely
60ml brandy
55g caster sugar
170g butter, softened
80g cream cheese, softened
275g caster sugar, extra
2 teaspoons vanilla extract
4 eggs
225g plain flour
1 teaspoon baking powder
1 teaspoon ground nutmeg
½ teaspoon salt
¼ teaspoon ground nutmeg,
    extra

brown butter frosting
80g butter
125g butter, extra, softened
350g icing sugar
1 teaspoon vanilla extract

1 Preheat oven to 160°C/140°C
fan-assisted. Grease a 20cm
round cake tin; line base and side
with baking parchment.
2 Combine apple, brandy and
sugar in a large saucepan; cook,
stirring, over medium heat until
sugar dissolves. Reduce heat to
low; cook, uncovered, stirring
occasionally, for 10 minutes or
until apple is tender. Cool.
3 Beat butter, cream cheese,
extra sugar and extract in a
medium bowl with an electric
mixer until pale and creamy.
Beat in eggs, one at a time, until
just combined. Add sifted flour,
baking powder, nutmeg and salt;
stir until just combined. Fold
apple through cake mixture.
Spoon mixture into tin.
4 Bake cake for 1 hour 35 minutes
or until a skewer inserted into the
centre comes out clean. Stand
cake in tin for 15 minutes before
turning, top-side down, onto a
baking-parchment-covered wire
rack to cool.
5 Make brown butter frosting.
6 Spread frosting on cake. Drizzle
with reserved browned butter;
dust with extra nutmeg.

brown butter frosting
Melt butter in a small frying
pan over medium heat; cook
for 2 minutes or until butter is
nut brown. Cool slightly. Beat
extra butter in a small bowl with
an electric mixer until pale and
creamy. Add sifted icing sugar,
in three batches, beating until
light and fluffy. Add extract and
2 tablespoons of the browned
butter; beat until combined.
Reserve remaining browned
butter.

prep + cook time 2 hours
(+ cooling time)
serves 10
tips It is best to pour the
remaining brown butter over the
cake just before serving or it will
set. You can reheat the butter in a
microwave on a low power setting
if necessary.
• Uniced cake can be made a
day ahead; store in an airtight
container at room temperature.

CHOCOLATE, PRUNE & ALMOND FUDGE CAKE

165g butter
4 eggs
210g pitted prunes
160ml brandy
165g dark eating chocolate
165g caster sugar
240g ground almonds

1 Preheat oven to 160°C/140°C fan-assisted. Grease 28cm closed springform cake tin; line base and side with baking parchment.

2 Chop prunes into small saucepan, add brandy; bring to the boil. Reduce heat, simmer, uncovered, 5 minutes; cool.

3 Break chocolate into medium heatproof bowl over saucepan of simmering water (don't let the water touch the base of the bowl); stir until smooth. Cool.

4 Beat butter and sugar in small bowl with electric mixer until light and fluffy. Beat in eggs, one at a time. Transfer mixture to large bowl; stir in prune mixture, ground almonds and chocolate.

5 Spread mixture into tin; bake cake about 45 minutes. Cool cake in tin.

6 Serve cake with cream.

prep + cook time 1 hour (+ cooling time)

serves 10

tips It's important to measure the closed springform tin; the measurement that appears on the base of the springform tin sometimes refers to the measurement of the tin when it is open.

• You could also use a 28cm PushPan for this recipe. To prepare the pan, oil the inside walls then push in the base. When the cake is ready, run a palette knife around the edges to loosen it before pushing it out.

• Cake will keep in an airtight container at room temperature for 3 days, or in the refrigerator for 1 week, or frozen for 2 months.

TIRAMISU ROULADE

2 tablespoons coffee-flavoured liqueur
60ml water
2 tablespoons caster sugar
1 tablespoon instant coffee granules
1 tablespoon boiling water
3 eggs
110g caster sugar, extra
75g plain flour
2 tablespoons flaked almonds

coffee liqueur cream
250g mascarpone
125ml double cream
2 tablespoons coffee-flavoured liqueur

1 Preheat oven to 220°C/200°C fan-assisted. Grease 25cm x 30cm swiss roll tin; line base and two long sides with baking parchment, extending paper 5cm over long sides.

2 Combine liqueur with the water and sugar in small saucepan; bring to a boil. Reduce heat; simmer, uncovered, without stirring, about 5 minutes or until syrup thickens slightly. Remove from heat, stir in half of the coffee; reserve syrup.

3 Dissolve remaining coffee in the boiling water.

4 Beat eggs and extra sugar in small bowl with electric mixer about 5 minutes or until sugar is dissolved and mixture is thick; transfer to large bowl, fold in dissolved coffee.

5 Sift flour twice onto a piece of baking parchment. Sift flour over egg mixture then fold gently into mixture. Spread sponge mixture into tin; sprinkle with almonds. Bake about 15 minutes.

6 Meanwhile, make coffee liqueur cream.

7 Place a piece of baking parchment cut the same size as swiss roll tin on worktop; sprinkle evenly with about 2 teaspoons of caster sugar. Turn sponge onto sugared paper; peel away lining paper. Using a serrated knife, cut away crisp edges from all sides of sponge. Roll sponge from long side, using paper as guide; cool.

8 Unroll sponge, brush with reserved syrup. Spread coffee liqueur cream over sponge then re-roll sponge. Cover roulade with cling film; refrigerate 30 minutes before serving.

coffee liqueur cream
Beat ingredients in small bowl with electric mixer until firm peaks form.

prep + cook time 55 minutes (+ refrigeration time)
serves 8
tip Use whatever coffee-flavoured liqueur you prefer in the cream filling, or you could use chocolate, almond, hazelnut, liquorice or even mint liqueur.

WALNUT CAKE WITH ESPRESSO MASCARPONE CREAM

125g butter, softened
150g demerara sugar
3 eggs, separated
200g self-raising flour
160g ground walnuts
160ml milk
90g honey
50g walnut halves, roasted

espresso mascarpone cream
250g mascarpone
1 tablespoon icing sugar
1 tablespoon instant coffee
  granules
1 tablespoon hot water

1 Preheat oven to 160°C/140°C fan-assisted. Grease deep 20cm round cake tin; line base and side with baking parchment.
2 Beat butter and sugar in a small bowl with an electric mixer until light and fluffy. Beat in egg yolks, one at a time, until combined. Transfer mixture to a large bowl; stir in sifted flour, ground walnuts and milk, in two batches.
3 Beat egg whites in a small bowl with an electric mixer until soft peaks form. Fold egg whites into cake mixture.
4 Spread mixture into tin. Bake about 50 minutes. Stand cake in tin 5 minutes before turning, top-side up, onto a wire rack to cool.
5 Meanwhile, make espresso mascarpone cream.
6 Using a serrated knife, split cake into two layers. Place bottom layer on a serving plate; spread with half the espresso cream; top with remaining layer. Warm the honey slightly. Spread top of cake with remaining espresso cream, scatter with walnut halves and drizzle with honey.

espresso mascarpone cream
Beat mascarpone and sifted icing sugar in a small bowl with a wooden spoon until combined. Dissolve coffee in the hot water in a small cup; fold into mascarpone mixture. Cover; refrigerate until ready to use.

prep + cook time 1 hour 30 minutes (+ refrigeration time)
serves 8

MILLIONAIRE'S SHORTBREAD

150g plain flour
110g light brown sugar
40g desiccated coconut
125g butter, melted
60g butter, extra
395g canned sweetened
  condensed milk
2 tablespoons golden syrup or
  treacle
185g dark eating chocolate,
  chopped coarsely
2 teaspoons vegetable oil

1 Preheat oven to 180°C/160°C fan-assisted. Grease a 20cm x 30cm rectangular tin; line base and long sides with baking parchment, extending the paper 5cm over sides.
2 Combine sifted flour, sugar and coconut in a medium bowl; stir in butter. Press mixture firmly over base of tin; bake slice about 15 minutes. Cool.
3 Place extra butter, condensed milk and syrup in a medium saucepan; stir over low heat until smooth. Pour mixture over base. Bake slice about 15 minutes or until golden brown. Cool.
4 Stir chocolate and oil in a medium heatproof bowl over a medium saucepan of simmering water until smooth. Spread chocolate mixture over slice. Refrigerate about 30 minutes or until set before cutting with a hot knife.

prep + cook time 55 minutes (+ refrigeration time)
makes 48
tip Shortbread will keep in an airtight container for up to a week. In hot weather, store the container in the refrigerator.

PISTACHIO & ROSEWATER LAYER CAKE

200g roasted unsalted shelled
   pistachios
250g butter, softened
330g caster sugar
2 teaspoons finely grated
   lemon rind
4 eggs
150g plain flour
75g self-raising flour
200g Greek-style natural yogurt

rosewater buttercream
250g butter, softened
2 teaspoons rosewater
480g icing sugar

1 Preheat oven to 170°C/150°C fan-assisted. Grease a deep 22cm round cake tin; line base and side with baking parchment.
2 Blend or process nuts until finely ground.
3 Beat butter, sugar and rind in a medium bowl with an electric mixer until light and fluffy. Beat in eggs, one at a time. Stir in sifted flours, yogurt and 100g of the ground nuts. Spread mixture into the tin.
4 Bake cake for about 1 hour 10 minutes. Stand in tin 5 minutes; turn, top-side up, onto a wire rack to cool.
5 Make rosewater buttercream.
6 Split cake in half. Place bottom layer, cut-side up, onto a serving plate; spread with one-third of the buttercream, top with remaining cake layer. Spread remaining buttercream all over cake. Sprinkle remaining ground nuts on top of cake.

rosewater buttercream
Beat butter and rosewater in a medium bowl with an electric mixer until as white as possible. Gradually beat in sifted icing sugar until smooth.

prep + cook time 2 hours
serves 12
tips Rosewater will vary in strength between brands. Start adding a small amount at a time and adjust to your taste. If you're using rosewater essence, start with 1 teaspoon.
• This cake will keep in an airtight container for up to 3 days.

VANILLA PEAR ALMOND CAKE

8 small firm ripe pears (800g)
625ml water
1 strip lemon rind
385g caster sugar
1 vanilla pod
125g butter, softened
3 eggs
160g soured cream
100g plain flour
100g self-raising flour
40g blanched almonds, roasted, chopped coarsely
40g dark eating chocolate, chopped coarsely
60g ground almonds

1 Peel pears, leaving stems intact.

2 Combine the water, rind and 220g of the sugar in medium saucepan. Split vanilla pod in half lengthways; scrape seeds into pan, then add pod. Stir over heat, without boiling, until sugar dissolves. Add pears; bring to the boil. Reduce heat; simmer, covered, 30 minutes or until pears are just tender. Transfer pears to medium bowl; bring syrup to the boil. Boil, uncovered, until syrup reduces by half. Cool completely.

3 Preheat oven to 160°C/140°C fan-assisted. Insert base of 23cm springform tin upside down in tin to give a flat base; grease tin.

4 Beat butter and remaining sugar in medium bowl with electric mixer until light and fluffy. Beat in eggs, one at a time; beat in soured cream. Stir in 2 tablespoons of the syrup, then sifted flours, almonds, chocolate and ground almonds.

5 Spread mixture into tin; place pears upright around edge of tin, gently pushing to the bottom.

6 Bake cake about 1 hour 35 minutes. Stand cake in tin 10 minutes; remove from tin. Serve cake warm, brushed with remaining syrup.

prep + cook time 2 hours 45 minutes (+ cooling time)
serves 8
tips The cooking time for the pears will vary slightly depending on their ripeness.

DECADENT MINTED CHOCOLATE CAKE

270g dark eating chocolate
80ml water
8 eggs
150g caster sugar
310ml double cream
½ teaspoon mint essence

dark chocolate ganache
160ml double cream
200g dark eating chocolate

1 Preheat oven to 180°C/160°C fan-assisted. Grease two 24cm x 32cm swiss roll tins; line bases with baking parchment.
2 Break chocolate into small saucepan, add the water; stir over low heat until smooth.
3 Separate eggs. Beat egg yolks and sugar in small bowl with electric mixer about 5 minutes or until pale and thick. Beat in chocolate mixture until combined. Transfer to large bowl.
4 Beat egg whites in large bowl with electric mixer until soft peaks form. Fold about one-third of the egg white into chocolate mixture; fold in remaining egg white.
5 Pour mixture evenly into tins; level surface. Bake sponges about 20 minutes. Carefully turn sponges onto baking-parchment-covered wire racks to cool; the sponges are thin and delicate, so remove the lining paper slowly to prevent the sponge pulling apart and breaking.
6 Whip cream and essence in small bowl with electric mixer until soft peaks form.
7 Place sponges on board; trim edges to make two rectangles of the same size. Halve each sponge lengthways. Place one rectangle of sponge on a serving plate; spread with one-third of the cream mixture (see tips), top with another layer of sponge. Repeat layering, finishing with a sponge layer. Refrigerate 30 minutes.

8 Meanwhile, make chocolate ganache. Spread ganache over top of sponge. Refrigerate about 30 minutes before serving.

dark chocolate ganache
Bring cream to the boil in medium saucepan; remove from heat. Break chocolate into pan; stir until smooth. Stand about 15 minutes or until ganache is spreadable.

prep + cook time 1 hour 15 minutes (+ refrigeration time)
serves 12
tips When spreading the cream mixture over the sponge, don't go too close to the edges, the cream will spread a little when you add the next layers.
• Cake will keep in an airtight container in the refrigerator for 5 days.

LEMON CAKE WITH LEMON MASCARPONE FROSTING

125g butter, softened
2 teaspoons finely grated lemon
    rind
275g caster sugar
3 eggs
225g self-raising flour
125ml milk
60ml lemon juice

lemon mascarpone frosting
250ml double cream
80g icing sugar
2 teaspoons finely grated
    lemon rind
170g mascarpone cheese

1 Preheat oven to 180°C/160°C
fan-assisted. Grease a deep 20cm
round cake tin; line base with
baking parchment.
2 Make lemon mascarpone
frosting; refrigerate, covered, until
required.
3 Beat butter, rind and sugar
in a small bowl with an electric
mixer until light and fluffy. Beat
in eggs, one at a time (mixture
might separate at this stage, but
will come together later); transfer
mixture to a large bowl. Stir in
sifted flour, milk and juice, in two
batches. Pour mixture into tin.
4 Bake cake about 50 minutes.
Stand in tin 5 minutes; turn, top-
side up, onto a wire rack to cool.
5 Split cake into three layers,
place one layer onto a serving
plate, cut-side up; spread with
one-third of the frosting. Repeat
layering process, finishing with
frosting.

lemon mascarpone frosting
Beat cream, sifted icing sugar
and rind in a small bowl with an
electric mixer until soft peaks
form. Fold cream mixture into
mascarpone.

prep + cook time 1 hour
20 minutes
serves 8
tips Grate the lemon for the
frosting before you extract the
juice for the cake mixture.
• Cake will keep in an airtight
container, in the refrigerator,
for up to 3 days.

HAZELNUT MUD CAKE
WITH FUDGE FROSTING

360g dark eating chocolate,
  chopped coarsely
225g butter, chopped coarsely
165g light brown sugar
180ml water
110g plain flour
35g self-raising flour
50g ground hazelnuts
2 eggs
80ml hazelnut-flavoured liqueur

fudge frosting
45g butter, chopped coarsely
75g light brown sugar
1 tablespoon water
2 tablespoons hazelnut-flavoured
  liqueur
160g icing sugar
2 tablespoons cocoa powder

1 Preheat oven to 150°C/130°C fan-assisted. Grease a deep 20cm round cake tin; line base and side with baking parchment.
2 Stir chocolate, butter, sugar and the water in a medium saucepan over low heat until smooth. Transfer to a medium bowl; cool 15 minutes.
3 Stir sifted flours, ground hazelnuts, eggs and liqueur into chocolate mixture. Pour mixture into tin.
4 Bake cake about 1 hour 35 minutes. Stand in tin 5 minutes; turn, top-side up, onto a wire rack to cool.
5 Meanwhile, make fudge frosting.
6 Spread cake with frosting.

fudge frosting
Stir butter, brown sugar and the water in a small saucepan over heat, without boiling, until sugar dissolves. Remove from heat; stir in liqueur. Sift icing sugar and cocoa into a small bowl; gradually stir in hot butter mixture until smooth. Cover; refrigerate about 15 minutes or until frosting thickens. Beat frosting with a wooden spoon until spreadable.

prep + cook time 2 hours (+ cooling and refrigeration time)
serves 12
tips We used Frangelico for this recipe, but you can use any hazelnut or chocolate-flavoured liqueur you prefer.
• This cake can be stored in an airtight container for up to 3 days. Unfrosted cake can be frozen for up to 3 months.

BANANA CARAMEL LAYER CAKE

185g butter, softened
175g caster sugar
3 eggs
335g self-raising flour
½ teaspoon bicarbonate of soda
2 large bananas, mashed
80ml milk
180ml double cream
395g canned caramel filling
1 large banana (230g), sliced
   thinly
1 tablespoon icing sugar

1 Preheat oven to 180°C/160°C fan-assisted. Grease a 24cm bundt tin or 24cm patterned silicone pan well with butter.
2 Beat butter and caster sugar in a small bowl with an electric mixer until light and fluffy. Beat in eggs, one at a time. Transfer mixture to a large bowl; stir in sifted dry ingredients, mashed banana and milk. Spread mixture into tin.
3 Bake cake about 40 minutes. Stand in tin 5 minutes; turn onto a wire rack to cool.
4 Beat cream in a small bowl with an electric mixer until firm peaks form.
5 Split cake into three layers. Spread bottom layer of cake with half the caramel; top with half the banana slices, then half the cream. Repeat next layer using remaining caramel, banana slices and cream. Replace top of cake. Dust with sifted icing sugar. Serve immediately.

prep + cook time 1 hour 10 minutes
serves 8
tips The bananas need to be overripe for this recipe.
• Plain cake can be frozen for up to 3 months.

MINI
CAKES & BAKES

FIG & WALNUT SQUARES

125g walnuts, roasted
6 egg whites
185g unsalted butter, melted
240g icing sugar
75g plain flour
2 teaspoons finely grated
  orange rind
1 tablespoon orange juice
4 dried figs (85g), sliced thinly
1 tablespoon icing sugar, extra

1 Preheat oven to 200°C/180°C fan-assisted. Grease a 20cm x 30cm rectangular tin; line base and sides with baking parchment, extending the paper 5cm over sides.
2 Process nuts until ground finely.
3 Whisk egg whites in a medium bowl with a fork until frothy. Stir in butter, sifted icing sugar and flour, rind, juice and ground nuts. Spread mixture in tin; top with slices of fig.
4 Bake about 25 minutes or until golden. Cool in tin. Dust with sifted extra icing sugar before cutting into pieces.

prep + cook time 40 minutes
makes 20
tip These squares will keep in an airtight container for up to 3 days. They can be frozen for up to 3 months.

LEMON MERINGUE SQUARES

90g butter, softened
2 tablespoons caster sugar
1 egg
150g plain flour
80g apricot jam

lemon topping
2 eggs
2 egg yolks
110g caster sugar
300ml double cream
1 tablespoon finely grated
    lemon rind
2 tablespoons lemon juice

meringue
3 egg whites
165g caster sugar

1 Preheat oven to 200°C/180°C fan-assisted. Grease base of 20cm x 30cm rectangular tin; line base and two long sides with baking parchment, extending paper 5cm over long sides.
2 Beat butter, sugar and egg in small bowl with electric mixer until pale in colour; stir in sifted flour, in two batches. Press dough over base of tin; prick several times with fork. Bake about 15 minutes or until browned lightly. Cool 20 minutes; spread base with jam.
3 Reduce oven temperature to 170°C/150°C fan-assisted.
4 Make lemon topping. Pour topping over base. Bake about 35 minutes or until set; cool 20 minutes. Roughen surface of topping with fork.
5 Increase oven temperature to 220°C/200°C fan-assisted.
6 Make meringue.
7 Spread meringue evenly over topping; bake about 3 minutes or until browned lightly. Cool in tin 20 minutes before cutting.

lemon topping
Place ingredients in medium bowl; whisk until combined.

meringue
Beat egg whites in small bowl with electric mixer until soft peaks form; gradually add sugar, beating until dissolved between additions.

prep + cook time 1 hour 20 minutes (+ cooling time)
makes 16

TINY COFFEE CAKES

125g butter, softened
110g demerara sugar
2 eggs, separated
3 teaspoons instant coffee
 granules
1 tablespoon hot water
100g self-raising flour
2 tablespoons milk
2 teaspoons sieved instant
 coffee powder, for sprinkling

coffee icing
2 teaspoons instant coffee
 granules
1 tablespoon hot water
160g icing sugar

1 Preheat oven to 160°C/140°C fan-assisted. Grease three 12-hole (20ml) mini muffin pans.
2 Beat butter and sugar in a medium bowl with an electric mixer until light and fluffy. Beat in egg yolks, one at a time, until combined. Stir coffee and the hot water in a small cup until coffee dissolves. Stir sifted flour, milk and coffee mixture into butter mixture.
3 Beat egg whites in a small bowl with an electric mixer until soft peaks form. Fold egg whites into cake mixture.
4 Spoon 2 teaspoons of mixture into each pan hole. Bake cakes about 20 minutes. Cool cakes in pans 5 minutes before turning, top-side down, onto a wire rack to cool.
5 Meanwhile, make coffee icing. Spread cakes with icing, allowing it to drip a little down the sides. Sprinkle cakes with a little sieved instant coffee powder.

coffee icing
Stir coffee and the hot water in a small cup until coffee dissolves. Sift icing sugar into a small bowl; gradually stir in the coffee until icing is smooth.

prep + cook time 50 minutes
makes 36

BUTTERSCOTCH MINI LOAVES WITH ROASTED RHUBARB

125g butter, softened
1 teaspoon vanilla extract
165g dark brown sugar
2 eggs
110g self-raising flour
110g plain flour
160ml milk
10g butter, melted
1 tablespoon dark brown sugar, extra
½ teaspoon mixed spice

roasted rhubarb
500g rhubarb, trimmed
30g butter, melted
2 tablespoons caster sugar

1 Preheat oven to 180°C/160°C fan-assisted.
2 Make roasted rhubarb.
3 Grease an 8-hole (180ml) mini loaf tin; line base and sides with baking parchment.
4 Beat softened butter, extract and sugar in a small bowl with an electric mixer until light and fluffy. Beat in eggs, one at a time. Transfer mixture to a large bowl; stir in sifted flours and milk, in two batches. Spoon mixture into tin holes.
5 Bake mini loaves for about 25 minutes. Stand in tin 5 minutes; turn, top-side up, onto a wire rack.
6 Brush top of hot mini loaves with melted butter; sprinkle with combined extra sugar and spice. Serve mini loaves warm, topped with rhubarb.

roasted rhubarb
Cut rhubarb into 6cm lengths. Place rhubarb in a small shallow baking dish with butter and sugar; toss to combine. Bake about 30 minutes or until rhubarb is tender but still holds its shape.

prep + cook time 1 hour 20 minutes
makes 8

ANGEL CAKES

90g butter, softened
110g caster sugar
2 eggs
½ teaspoon vanilla extract
150g self-raising flour
2 tablespoons milk
80g desiccated coconut
125ml double cream
100g raspberry jam

chocolate icing
15g butter
80ml milk
320g icing sugar
25g cocoa powder

1 Preheat oven to 180°C/160°C fan-assisted. Line a 12-hole (80ml) muffin pan with paper cases.
2 Beat butter, sugar, eggs, extract, sifted flour and milk in a small bowl with an electric mixer on low speed until ingredients are just combined. Increase speed to medium; beat until mixture has changed to a paler colour. Spoon mixture into paper cases; smooth surface.
3 Bake cakes for 20 minutes. Stand in tin 5 minutes; turn, top-side up, onto a wire rack to cool. Remove paper cases from cakes.
4 Make chocolate icing.
5 Dip cakes in icing; drain off excess, toss cakes in coconut. Stand cakes on wire rack until set.
6 Meanwhile, beat cream in a small bowl until firm peaks form.
7 Cut cakes as desired; fill with jam and cream.

chocolate icing
Melt butter in a medium heatproof bowl over a medium saucepan of simmering water. Stir in milk and sifted icing sugar and cocoa until icing is of a coating consistency.

prep + cook time 1 hour (+ standing time)
makes 12
tip Cakes will keep in an airtight container in the refrigerator for up to 2 days. Uniced cakes can be frozen for up to 3 months.

UPSIDE DOWN APRICOT CAKES WITH ORANGE SYRUP

125g butter
2 eggs
2 teaspoons finely grated
  orange rind
150g caster sugar
150g soft dried apricot halves
225g self-raising flour
190g greek-style natural yogurt
2 tablespoons orange juice

orange syrup
220g caster sugar
80ml orange juice
2 tablespoons water

1 Preheat oven to 180°C/160°C fan-assisted. Grease 18 holes of two 12-hole (80ml) muffin pans.
2 Beat butter, rind and sugar in small bowl with electric mixer until light and fluffy. Beat in eggs, one at a time.
3 Place an apricot half in each pan hole, rounded-side down.
4 Transfer butter mixture to large bowl; stir in sifted flour, yogurt and juice, in two batches.
5 Divide mixture into pan holes. Bake about 25 minutes.
6 Meanwhile, make orange syrup.
7 Let cakes stand in pans 5 minutes before turning onto wire rack over tray. Pour hot syrup over hot cakes.

orange syrup
Combine ingredients in small saucepan; stir over heat, without boiling, until sugar dissolves. Bring to the boil. Boil, uncovered, without stirring, 2 minutes.

prep + cook time 50 minutes
makes 18
tip Cakes will keep in an airtight container at room temperature for 2 days, or in the refrigerator for 1 week.

GLAZED ROSEWATER MADELEINES

125g butter, melted
1 tablespoon plain flour
2 eggs
75g caster sugar
2 teaspoons rosewater
1 teaspoon vanilla bean paste
100g plain flour, extra
¼ teaspoon baking powder

glacé icing
160g icing sugar
1 teaspoon butter
2 tablespoons lemon juice,
    approximately
pink food colouring

1 Preheat oven to 200°C/180°C fan-assisted. Brush two 12-hole (30ml) madeleine tins with 1 tablespoon of the melted butter. Dust with the flour; shake out excess.
2 Beat eggs, sugar, rosewater and paste in a small bowl with an electric mixer for about 5 minutes or until thick and creamy.
3 Meanwhile, sift extra flour and baking powder twice onto a piece of baking parchment. Sift flour mixture over egg mixture; fold into egg mixture with remaining melted butter. Drop tablespoons of mixture into tin holes.
4 Bake madeleines for about 10 minutes. Stand in tins 2 minutes; turn onto a wire rack to cool.
5 Meanwhile, make glacé icing.
6 Dip one end of each madeleine into icing; place on a baking-parchment-covered wire rack 5 minutes or until set.

glacé icing
Sift icing sugar into a small heatproof bowl; stir in butter and enough juice to make a thick paste. Place the bowl over a small saucepan of simmering water; stir until icing is of a pouring consistency (do not overheat). Tint pink with colouring.

prep + cook time 35 minutes (+ standing time)
makes 24
tip Madeleines are best made and eaten on the same day.

ORANGE & WHITE CHOCOLATE PETITS FOURS

180g butter, softened
165g caster sugar
3 teaspoons finely grated
    orange rind
3 eggs
125ml orange juice
225g self-raising flour
2 tablespoons plain flour
125ml double cream
180g white eating chocolate,
    chopped finely
2 x 5cm strips orange rind
125ml boiling water

1 Preheat oven to 180°C/160°C fan-assisted. Grease a 20cm x 30cm rectangular tin; line base and sides with baking parchment, extending the paper 5cm over sides.
2 Beat butter, sugar and grated rind in a small bowl with electric mixer until light and fluffy. Beat in eggs, one at a time. Stir in juice and sifted flours. Spread mixture into tin.
3 Bake cake about 35 minutes. Stand in tin 10 minutes; transfer to a wire rack to cool. Using a 3.5cm cutter, cut 28 rounds from cake. Discard excess cake.
4 Bring cream to the boil in a small saucepan. Remove from heat; pour over chocolate in a small bowl, stir until smooth. Stand about 20 minutes or until thickened.
5 Slice strips of rind thinly; place in a small bowl with the boiling water. Soak 30 seconds; drain. Transfer rind to a small bowl of iced water; drain.
6 Place cake rounds on a wire rack over a baking-parchment-lined tray; spread ganache on cakes, top with rind. Stand until set.

prep + cook time 55 minutes (+ standing time)
makes 28
tips Petit fours can be served in mini paper cases.
• You could use candied orange peel instead of the thinly sliced orange rind.
• Petit fours are best made on the day of serving.

RASPBERRY ALMOND PETITS FOURS

125g butter, softened
165g caster sugar
3 eggs
75g plain flour
35g self-raising flour
60g ground almonds
80g soured cream
150g fresh raspberries
32 ready-made icing flowers

icing
400g icing sugar
2 tablespoons lemon juice
1½ tablespoons boiling water,
   approximately

1 Preheat oven to 180°C/160°C fan-assisted. Grease a 20cm x 30cm rectangular tin; line base and sides with baking parchment, extending the paper 5cm over sides.
2 Beat butter and sugar in a small bowl with an electric mixer until light and fluffy. Beat in eggs, one at a time. Stir in sifted flours, ground almonds, soured cream and raspberries. Spread mixture into tin.
3 Bake cake about 40 minutes. Stand in tin 10 minutes; transfer to a wire rack to cool. Using a serrated knife, trim and discard edges of cake. Cut cake into 32 squares.
4 Make icing.
5 Place cake squares on a wire rack over a baking-parchment-lined tray; spread or drizzle icing over squares. Top with icing flowers; stand until set.

icing
Stir ingredients in a medium bowl to a smooth paste (add a little extra water for a thinner consistency if you like).

prep + cook time 55 minutes (+ standing time)
makes 32
tips Petits fours can be served in mini paper cases.
• You could top the petit fours with fresh raspberries instead of the icing flowers.
• Petits fours are best made on the day of serving.

MINI CHOC-CHIP FRIANDS

3 egg whites
90g butter, melted
60g ground almonds
120g icing sugar
35g plain flour
100g dark eating chocolate,
    chopped finely
60ml double cream
100g dark eating chocolate,
    chopped coarsely, extra

1 Preheat oven to 180°C/160°C fan-assisted. Grease 18 holes of two 12-hole (20ml) mini muffin pans.
2 Whisk egg whites in medium bowl with a fork. Stir in butter, ground almonds, sifted icing sugar and flour until combined. Stir in chopped chocolate. Spoon mixture into pan holes.
3 Bake friands about 15 minutes. Turn, top-side up, onto wire racks to cool.
4 Place cream and extra chocolate in a medium heatproof bowl over a medium saucepan of simmering water; stir until smooth. Stand until thickened. Spread chocolate mixture on top of friands.

prep + cook time 40 minutes (+ standing time)
makes 18
tip Friands will keep in an airtight container in the refrigerator for up to 3 days. Uniced friands can be frozen for up to 3 months.

WHITE CHOCOLATE LAMINGTONS

6 eggs
150g caster sugar
80g white eating chocolate,
  chopped finely
75g plain flour
50g self-raising flour
50g cornflour
150g desiccated coconut
100g white eating chocolate,
  grated finely

icing
640g icing sugar
180ml milk

1 Preheat oven to 180°C/160°C fan-assisted. Grease a 20cm x 30cm rectangular tin; line base and sides with baking parchment, extending the paper 5cm over sides.

2 Beat eggs in a medium bowl with an electric mixer about 10 minutes or until thick and creamy. Gradually add sugar, beating until sugar dissolves. Fold in chopped chocolate and triple-sifted flours. Spread mixture into tin.

3 Bake cake about 35 minutes. Turn cake onto a baking-parchment-covered wire rack to cool; refrigerate until required.

4 Make icing.

5 Cut cake into 35 squares; dip each square in icing, drain off excess. Toss squares in combined coconut and grated chocolate; place on a wire rack to set.

icing
Sift icing sugar into a medium heatproof bowl; stir in milk. Place over a medium saucepan of simmering water; stir until icing is of a coating consistency.

prep + cook time 1 hour
(+ refrigeration and standing time)
makes 18
tip Lamingtons can be made 1 day ahead of serving. Keep them in an airtight container in the refrigerator. The un-cut cake can be frozen for up to 3 months.

FROU FROU CAKES

125g butter, softened
220g caster sugar
3 eggs
75g plain flour
35g self-raising flour
40g desiccated coconut
80g soured cream
155g frozen raspberries (see tip)
50g toasted coconut chips
15 fresh raspberries, halved

cream cheese frosting
60g butter, softened
155g cream cheese, softened
2 teaspoons coconut extract
480g icing sugar

1 Preheat oven to 180°C/160°C fan-assisted. Line a 12-hole (80ml) muffin pan with paper cases.
2 Beat butter, sugar and eggs in a small bowl with an electric mixer until light and fluffy. Stir in sifted flours, desiccated coconut, soured cream and frozen raspberries. Spoon mixture into paper cases; smooth surface.
3 Bake cakes about 40 minutes. Stand in pan 5 minutes; turn, top-side up, onto a wire rack to cool. Remove paper cases from cakes.
4 Make cream cheese frosting.
5 Spread top and side of cakes with frosting; decorate with coconut chips and fresh raspberries.

cream cheese frosting
Beat butter, cream cheese and extract in a small bowl with an electric mixer until light and fluffy; gradually beat in sifted icing sugar.

prep + cook time 1 hour
makes 12

tips Do not thaw the frozen raspberries as their colour will bleed into the cake.
• These cakes are best made on the day of serving. Unfrosted cakes can be frozen for up to 3 months.
• Toasted coconut chips are available from health food stores and online.

CELEBRATION
CAKES & BAKES

RASPBERRY LAYERED BUTTERFLY CAKE

185g white eating chocolate, chopped coarsely
90g unsalted butter, chopped coarsely
250ml buttermilk
275g caster sugar
3 eggs
1 teaspoon vanilla extract
150g plain flour
75g self-raising flour
½ teaspoon bicarbonate of soda
125g Bright White Candy Melts

fluffy mock cream frosting
80ml milk
160ml water
440g caster sugar
2 teaspoons gelatine
80ml water, extra
500g unsalted butter, softened
2 teaspoons vanilla extract
80g raspberry jam, warmed, strained, cooled
pink food colouring

1 Preheat oven to 150°C/130°C fan-assisted. Grease two 17cm round cake tins; line bases and sides with baking parchment, extending the paper 5cm above sides.
2 Stir chocolate, butter and buttermilk in a medium saucepan over low heat until smooth. Transfer to a large bowl; cool 10 minutes.
3 Whisk sugar, eggs and extract into chocolate mixture. Whisk in sifted dry ingredients until mixture is smooth and glossy. Divide mixture evenly into tins.
4 Bake cakes for about 1 hour. Stand in tins 5 minutes; turn, top-side up, onto wire racks to cool.
5 Make fluffy mock cream frosting. Transfer half the frosting to a medium bowl, stir in jam; tint pink with colouring.
6 Draw butterflies onto baking parchment (we used one large, one medium and five small butterflies); place parchment, marked-side down, onto an oven tray.
7 Place Candy Melts in a small heatproof bowl over a small saucepan of simmering water; stir until melted. Tint melted Melts pink; spoon into a piping bag. Pipe around and inside butterfly shapes on tray; stand at room temperature until set.

8 Split cakes in half; sandwich cakes with pink frosting on a cake stand or prepared cake board (see tips). Spread cake all over with remaining plain frosting. Position butterflies on cake.

fluffy mock cream frosting
Stir milk, the water and sugar in a medium saucepan over low heat, without boiling, until sugar dissolves. Sprinkle gelatine over the extra water in a cup, add to pan; stir syrup until gelatine is dissolved. Cool to room temperature. Beat butter and extract in a medium bowl with an electric mixer until as white as possible. With motor operating, gradually pour in cold syrup in thin, steady stream; beat until light and fluffy. Mixture will thicken more on standing.

prep + cook time 2 hours 20 minutes (+ cooling and standing time)
serves 10
tips You will need one 20cm round board for this cake.
• The cake can be baked 2 days ahead (or baked then frozen for up to 3 months). Fill and decorate the cake on the day of serving.
• Candy Melts, available from Lakeland, are perfect for melting, moulding, dipping and drizzling.

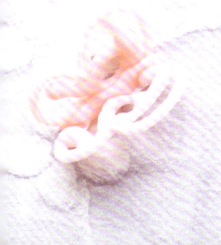

POLKA DOT CAKE

250g unsalted butter, softened
550g caster sugar
2 teaspoons vanilla extract
6 eggs
225g plain flour
225g self-raising flour
250ml milk
315g Bright White Candy Melts
pink, yellow, blue and green food
    colourings

white chocolate ganache
500g white eating chocolate,
    chopped coarsely
375ml double cream

1 Preheat oven to 140°C/120°C fan-assisted. Grease two deep 22cm round cake tins; line bases and sides with baking parchment, extending the paper 5cm above sides.
2 Beat butter, sugar, extract, eggs, sifted flours and milk in a large bowl with an electric mixer on low speed until combined. Increase speed to medium; beat about 2 minutes or until mixture is smooth and changed to a paler colour. Spread mixture evenly into tins; tap gently on the worktop to release large air bubbles.
3 Bake cakes about 1 hour. Stand in tins 5 minutes; turn, top-side up, onto wire racks to cool.
4 Meanwhile, make white chocolate ganache.
5 Place Candy Melts in a small heatproof bowl over a small saucepan of simmering water; stir until melted. Divide between four small bowls; tint with colourings.
6 Working with one colour at a time, spoon into small piping bags. Pipe small, medium and large discs onto a baking-parchment-lined tray; tap tray gently on the worktop to flatten rounds. Stand at room temperature until set.

7 Level top of cakes. Place one cake on a cake stand or prepared cake board (see tips); spread with one-third of the ganache, top with other cake. Spread remaining ganache all over cake. Decorate with candy discs.

white chocolate ganache
Stir ingredients in a large heatproof bowl over a large saucepan of simmering water until smooth. Cover; refrigerate about 3 hours or until thick. Beat ganache in a large bowl with electric mixer until firm peaks form.

prep + cook time 1 hour 30 minutes (+ refrigeration and standing time)
serves 14
tips Use small piping bags without a tube or strong plastic bags – snip a tiny corner from the bag for easy piping.
• You will need one 30cm round board for this cake.
• This cake can be made a day ahead; keep in the refrigerator. Plain cakes can be frozen for up to 3 months.
• Candy Melts, available from Lakeland, are perfect for melting, moulding, dipping and drizzling.

SOURED CREAM CHOCOLATE CAKE

185g dark eating chocolate,
  chopped coarsely
35g cocoa powder
410ml boiling water
250g unsalted butter, softened
440g dark brown sugar
4 eggs
1 teaspoon vanilla extract
180g soured cream
150g plain flour
150g self-raising flour
1 teaspoon bicarbonate of soda

milk chocolate ganache
700g milk eating chocolate,
  chopped coarsely
410ml double cream

1 Preheat oven to 140°C/120°C fan-assisted. Grease two deep 20cm round cake tins: line bases and sides with baking parchment.
2 Stir chocolate, sifted cocoa and the water in a medium saucepan over low heat until smooth. Transfer mixture to a large bowl; cool 15 minutes.
3 Add butter, sugar, eggs, extract, soured cream and sifted dry ingredients to chocolate mixture; beat on low speed with electric mixer until combined. Increase speed to medium; beat about 3 minutes or until mixture is smooth and changed to a paler colour. Spread mixture evenly into tins.
4 Bake cakes about 1 hour 15 minutes. Stand in tins 5 minutes; turn, top-side up, onto wire racks to cool.
5 Meanwhile, make milk chocolate ganache.
6 Split cakes in half; sandwich cakes using about 6 tablespoons of the ganache between each layer. Position cake on a cake stand or prepared cake board (see tips), secure with a little ganache. Spread cake all over with remaining ganache.

milk chocolate ganache
Stir ingredients in a large heatproof bowl over a large saucepan of simmering water until smooth. Cover; refrigerate 3 hours or until thick. Beat ganache in a large bowl with an electric mixer until firm peaks form.

prep + cook time 1 hour 45 minutes (+ cooling and refrigeration time)
serves 10
tips You will need one 25cm round board for this cake.
• The cake and ganache can be made a day ahead. Store cake in an airtight container. Whip ganache and assemble cake up to an hour before serving. Plain cakes can be frozen for up to 3 months.

LEMON CURD MERINGUE CAKE WITH TOFFEE-DIPPED BLUEBERRIES

150g almonds
4 egg whites
220g caster sugar
125g white eating chocolate, grated coarsely
625ml double cream (see tip)

lemon curd
250g chilled butter, chopped coarsely
2 eggs, beaten lightly
160ml lemon juice
300g caster sugar
2 egg yolks

toffee-dipped blueberries
220g granulated sugar
125ml water
125g fresh blueberries

1 Make lemon curd.
2 Preheat oven to 160°C/140°C fan-assisted. Grease a 24cm closed springform cake tin; insert base of tin upside down to make cake easier to remove. Line base with baking parchment.
3 Spread nuts, in a single layer, on an oven tray; roast, uncovered, about 12 minutes or until skins begin to split. Cool. Chop nuts finely.
4 Beat egg whites and 55g of the sugar in a small bowl with an electric mixer until firm peaks form. Add remaining sugar; beat on high speed about 5 minutes or until sugar is dissolved. Fold in chocolate and nuts. Spread mixture into tin.
5 Bake meringue for about 40 minutes. Cool in tin.
6 Beat half the cream in a small bowl with an electric mixer until soft peaks form; fold in curd. Spoon curd mixture onto meringue. Refrigerate several hours or overnight until firm.
7 Before serving, make toffee-dipped blueberries. Spoon remaining cream onto cake; top with toffee-dipped berries. Serve immediately.

lemon curd
Place butter in a medium saucepan; strain egg through a sieve into pan. Add remaining ingredients; stir over low heat, without boiling, about 10 minutes or until mixture thickly coats the back of a spoon. Transfer curd to a medium heatproof bowl; refrigerate until cold.

toffee-dipped blueberries
Stir sugar and the water in a small saucepan over medium heat until sugar is dissolved. Bring to the boil; boil, without stirring, until sugar has thickened and turns a caramel colour. Push a wooden toothpick into each blueberry. Remove toffee from heat; allow bubbles to subside. Working with one blueberry at a time, holding by the toothpick, dip berry into thickened toffee. Hold berry above toffee so a trail of toffee falls from the berry. Hold upside down until starting to set. You may need to reheat the toffee if it starts to thicken too much.

prep + cook time 1 hour 45 minutes (+ refrigeration time)
serves 12
tip You can use two 300ml cartons of cream for this recipe; one for the curd mixture and one to spoon onto the cake.

MIXED BERRY, HAZELNUT & WHITE CHOCOLATE CAKE

200g white eating chocolate
250g butter
385g caster sugar
250ml water
150g plain flour
75g self-raising flour
50g ground hazelnuts
1 teaspoon vanilla extract
2 eggs
150g frozen mixed berries

whipped white chocolate ganache
250g white eating chocolate
60g butter
125ml double cream

sugared berries
150g fresh mixed berries
1 egg white
75g granulated sugar

1 Preheat oven to 160°C/140°C fan-assisted. Lightly grease deep 22cm round cake tin.
2 Break chocolate into medium saucepan, add chopped butter, sugar and the water; stir over low heat, until smooth. Transfer mixture to large bowl; cool 10 minutes.
3 Whisk sifted flours, ground hazelnuts, extract and eggs into chocolate mixture until combined; gently stir through berries.
4 Pour mixture into tin. Bake cake about 1 hour 50 minutes. Stand cake in tin 10 minutes before turning, top-side up, onto wire rack to cool.
5 Meanwhile, make whipped white chocolate ganache and sugared berries.
6 Place cake on serving plate, spread all over with ganache; top with berries.

whipped white chocolate ganache
Break chocolate into medium saucepan, add butter and cream; stir over low heat until smooth. Transfer mixture to small bowl; cool. Beat mixture with electric mixer until fluffy.

sugared berries
Brush berries with egg white; toss gently in sugar. Place on a tray to dry.

prep + cook time 2 hours 30 minutes (+ standing time)
serves 12
tip Cake will keep for up to a week in an airtight container in the refrigerator. Unfrosted cake can be frozen for 2 months.

ORANGE BLOSSOM & RASPBERRY ANGEL FOOD CAKE

125g frozen raspberries, thawed
75g plain flour
75g cornflour
275g caster sugar
12 egg whites
1 teaspoon cream of tartar
2 teaspoons orange flower water
3 tablespoons edible flowers

orange blossom icing
320g icing sugar
¼ teaspoon orange blossom water
60ml strained lemon juice

1 Preheat oven to 180°C/160°C fan-assisted. Adjust oven shelf to lowest position.
2 Push raspberries through a fine sieve into a small bowl; discard seeds. Sift flours and 55g sugar together five times.
3 Beat egg whites in a large bowl with an electric mixer until foamy; beat in cream of tartar. Gradually add remaining sugar, beating until sugar dissolves and mixture is very thick and glossy. Whisk in orange blossom water. Sift one-third of the flour mixture on meringue; gently fold through using a balloon whisk. Repeat with remaining flour mixture, in batches.
4 Transfer one-third of the cake mixture to a medium bowl; fold in raspberry purée. Carefully fold raspberry mixture into remaining cake mixture, swirling to create a marbled effect. Spoon mixture into an ungreased 25cm ring tin; smooth surface.
5 Bake cake for 30 minutes or until cake springs back when pressed lightly with a finger.
6 Place a piece of baking parchment, just larger than the tin on a work surface. Immediately turn hot tin upside-down on the paper; leave to cool completely in this position. The cake will drop when cold; if not, you may need to run a spatula around the cake to release it.
7 Make orange blossom icing.
8 Drizzle cake with icing; decorate with flowers.

orange blossom icing
Sift icing sugar into a small bowl; stir in orange flower water and enough of the juice to form an icing the consistency of honey.

prep + cook time 50 minutes (+ cooling time)
serves 12
tips Taste and adjust the icing with more orange flower water if necessary.
• Edible flowers, including lavender, pansies, violets, nasturtiums and rose petals, are a lovely way to decorate cakes. It is best to pick them fresh from your garden on the day you are going to use them and make sure they have not been treated with chemicals.
• You could decorate the cake with 125g fresh raspberries instead of the flowers.
• The cake is best made on day of serving.

SILVER ANNIVERSARY CUPCAKES

250ml vegetable oil
300g light brown sugar
3 eggs
540g coarsely grated carrot
  (3 large carrots)
110g walnuts, coarsely chopped
375g self-raising flour
½ teaspoon bicarbonate of soda
2 teaspoons mixed spice

butter cream
125g butter, softened
240g icing sugar
2 tablespoons milk
white food colouring

decorations
silver balls
18 x 20cm lengths pale pink
  ribbon

1 Preheat oven to 180°C/160°C fan-assisted. Line 18 holes of two 12-hole (80ml) muffin pans with paper cases.
2 Beat oil, sugar and eggs in small bowl with electric mixer until thick. Transfer mixture to large bowl; stir in carrot, nuts, then sifted dry ingredients. Divide mixture between the paper cases.
3 Bake cakes about 30 minutes. Stand in pans 5 minutes before turning, top-side up, onto wire racks to cool.
4 Make butter cream. Spread cakes with butter cream. Position silver balls on each cake to form the number '25'; gently push silver balls into butter cream. Tie ribbons in bows around each cupcake.

butter cream
Beat butter in small bowl with electric mixer until as white as possible; beat in sifted icing sugar and milk, in two batches. Tint butter cream white with food colouring.

prep + cook time 1 hour 10 minutes
makes 18
tip These cupcakes can be adapted for any anniversary or birthday by varying the number on the cakes and colour of the decorations.

GRADUATION DAY CUPCAKES

60g dark eating chocolate,
  chopped coarsely
160ml water
90g butter, softened
220g light brown sugar
2 eggs
100g self-raising flour
2 tablespoons cocoa powder
40g ground almonds

white chocolate ganache
125ml double cream
345g white eating chocolate,
  chopped coarsely

decorations
12 Maltesers
12 dark chocolate squares
20cm piece black liquorice
  bootlace
30g dark eating chocolate,
  melted

1 Preheat oven to 170°C/150°C fan-assisted. Line 12-hole (80ml) muffin pan with paper cases.
2 Stir chocolate and the water in small saucepan over low heat until smooth.
3 Beat butter, sugar and eggs in small bowl with electric mixer until light and fluffy. Stir in sifted flour and cocoa, ground almonds and warm chocolate mixture. Divide the mixture between the paper cases.
4 Bake cakes about 25 minutes. Stand in pan 5 minutes before turning, top-side up, onto wire rack to cool.
5 Make white chocolate ganache. Spread cakes with ganache.
6 Place a Malteser in centre of each cake, position chocolate square on Malteser to make a mortarboard. Cut thin strips, about 4cm long, from liquorice bootlace; split the end of each into fine strips to make tassels. Attach a tassel to each mortarboard with a tiny dab of the melted chocolate.

white chocolate ganache
Bring cream to the boil in small saucepan; remove from heat. When bubbles subside, add chocolate; stir until smooth. Cool 15 minutes.

prep + cook time 1 hour
makes 12

LEMON MERINGUE
WEDDING CUPCAKES

125g butter, softened
2 teaspoons finely grated
   lemon rind
150g caster sugar
2 eggs
80ml milk
60g desiccated coconut
185g self-raising flour

lemon curd
4 egg yolks
75g caster sugar
2 teaspoons finely grated
   lemon rind
60ml lemon juice
45g butter

coconut meringue
4 egg whites
220g caster sugar
80g desiccated coconut,
   chopped finely

1 Make lemon curd.
2 Preheat oven to 180°C/160°C fan-assisted. Line 12-hole (80ml) muffin pan with paper cases.
3 Beat butter, rind, sugar and eggs in small bowl with electric mixer until light and fluffy. Stir in milk and coconut, then sifted flour. Divide mixture into paper cases; smooth surface.
4 Bake cakes about 20 minutes. Stand in pan 5 minutes before turning, top-side up, onto wire rack to cool.
5 Meanwhile, increase oven temperature to 220°C/200°C fan-assisted.
6 Cut a 2cm deep hole in the centre of each cake, fill with curd; discard cake tops.
7 Make coconut meringue. Spoon meringue into a piping bag fitted with a 1cm plain tube. Pipe meringue onto cake tops; place cakes on oven tray.
8 Bake in oven 5 minutes or until meringue is browned lightly.

lemon curd
Combine ingredients in small heatproof bowl over small saucepan of simmering water, stirring constantly, until mixture thickens slightly and coats the back of a spoon. Remove from heat. Cover tightly; refrigerate curd until cold.

coconut meringue
Beat egg whites in small bowl with electric mixer until soft peaks form; gradually add sugar, beating until sugar dissolves. Fold in coconut.

prep + cook time 1 hour `
(+ refrigeration time)
makes 12
tip This recipe also makes six large cupcakes (180ml); bake for about 25 minutes.

BABY FEET CUPCAKES

125g butter, chopped coarsely
100g white eating chocolate, chopped coarsely
150g light brown sugar
90g golden syrup
160ml milk
150g plain flour
50g self-raising flour
1 egg

butter cream
90g butter, softened
240g icing sugar
1 tablespoon milk
white food colouring

decorations
12 small yellow jelly beans
yellow writing icing

1 Preheat oven to 170°C/150°C fan-assisted. Line 12-hole (80ml) muffin pan with paper cases.
2 Stir butter, chocolate, sugar, syrup and milk in small saucepan over low heat until smooth. Transfer mixture to medium bowl; cool 15 minutes.
3 Whisk sifted flours into chocolate mixture, then whisk in egg.
4 Divide mixture between paper cases. Bake cupcakes about 30 minutes. Stand in pan 5 minutes before turning, top-side up, onto wire rack to cool.
5 Make butter cream. Spread cakes with butter cream.
6 Split jelly beans in half lengthways, position on cakes. Use writing icing to pipe toes.

butter cream
Beat butter in small bowl with electric mixer until as white as possible; beat in sifted icing sugar and milk, in two batches. Tint butter cream white with food colouring.

prep + cook time 1 hour (+ cooling time)
makes 12
tips You can use any colour jelly beans you like. Choose a writing icing to match the colour of the jelly beans.
• White food colouring is available from cake decorating shops and online.

FESTIVE
CAKES & BAKES

RICH CHOCOLATE FRUIT CAKE

2 x 425g cans pitted black
  cherries in syrup
150g raisins, chopped
120g pitted dates, chopped
  finely
80g sultanas
95g pitted prunes, chopped
  finely
200g dried figs, chopped finely
250ml marsala
120g pecans
185g butter, softened
2 teaspoons finely grated
  orange rind
275g dark brown sugar
3 eggs
185g plain flour
75g self-raising flour
2 tablespoons cocoa powder
2 teaspoons mixed spice
100g dark eating chocolate,
  chopped finely

dark chocolate ganache
200g dark eating chocolate,
  chopped coarsely
125ml double cream

1 Drain cherries; reserve 80ml syrup. Quarter cherries. Combine cherries with remaining fruit, 180ml of the marsala and reserved cherry syrup in large bowl. Cover; stand overnight.
2 Preheat oven to 150°C/130°C fan-assisted. Line deep 22cm round cake tin with two thicknesses of baking parchment, extending the paper 5cm above side.
3 Process half the nuts until finely ground; chop remaining nuts coarsely.
4 Beat butter, rind and sugar in small bowl with electric mixer until combined. Beat in eggs, one at a time. Stir egg mixture into fruit mixture; stir in sifted dry ingredients, chocolate and ground and chopped nuts.
5 Spread mixture into tin; bake about 3 hours. Brush hot cake with remaining marsala; cover with foil, cool in tin overnight.
6 Make ganache.
7 Spread cake with ganache; top with chocolate decoration. Dust with sifted icing sugar to serve, if you like.

dark chocolate ganache
Stir ingredients in small saucepan over low heat until smooth. Refrigerate, stirring occasionally, about 20 minutes or until spreadable.

prep + cook time 3 hours 50 minutes (+ standing, cooling and refrigeration time)
serves 20
tip We roughly painted a branch of real holly with melted dark chocolate to make the inedible decoration on the cake.

CHRISTMAS MUFFINS

450g self-raising flour
100g butter, chopped
220g caster sugar
310ml buttermilk
1 egg, beaten lightly
250g coarsely chopped mixed
   glacé fruit
250g ready-made white icing
2 tablespoons apricot jam,
   warmed, strained
1 tablespoon icing sugar
   for dusting

1 Preheat oven to 200°C/180°C fan-assisted. Line a 12-hole (80ml) muffin pan with paper cases.
2 Sift flour into medium bowl; rub in butter. Gently stir in sugar, buttermilk and egg, then stir in the glacé fruit.
3 Spoon mixture into pan holes; bake muffins about 20 minutes. Stand in pan 5 minutes; turn, top-side up, onto wire rack to cool.
4 Roll icing out to 5mm thick; cut out 12 x 4.5cm stars. Brush tops of muffins with jam; top with icing stars. Dust with a little sifted icing sugar, if you like.

prep + cook time 40 minutes
makes 12

LIGHT FRUIT CAKE
WITH ALMOND CRUMBLE

160g sultanas

85g raisins, chopped coarsely

125g glacé peaches, chopped coarsely

125g glacé apricots, chopped coarsely

60g glacé orange rind, chopped coarsely

50g red glacé cherries, chopped coarsely

125ml orange-flavoured liqueur

185g butter, softened

220g caster sugar

2 teaspoons vanilla extract

2 eggs

80g soured cream

90g ground almonds

110g plain flour

50g self-raising flour

almond crumble

75g plain flour

60g butter

2 tablespoons light brown sugar

90g marzipan or almond paste

40g flaked almonds

1 Combine fruit and liqueur in a large bowl. Cover; stand about 1 hour or until most of the liquid is absorbed. Stir well.

2 Make almond crumble.

3 Preheat oven to 150°C/130°C fan-assisted. Grease a deep 14cm x 23cm loaf tin; line base and sides with two thicknesses of baking parchment, extending the paper 5cm above sides.

4 Beat butter, sugar and extract in a small bowl with an electric mixer until combined. Beat in eggs, one at a time; beat in soured cream. Stir butter mixture into fruit mixture, then stir in ground almonds and sifted flours. Spoon mixture into tin; smooth surface. Sprinkle with almond crumble.

5 Bake cake about 1 hour 45 minutes. Cover with foil; cool cake in tin.

almond crumble

Place flour in a medium bowl; rub in butter until crumbly. Stir in sugar, crumbled marzipan and nuts.

prep + cook time 2 hours 15 minutes (+ standing time)

serves 12

tips Use Cointreau, Grand Marnier or curaçao for a citrus-flavoured liqueur.

• Cake will keep in an airtight container at room temperature for up to 4 weeks. It can be frozen for up to 3 months.

PANETTONE

200g mixed dried fruit
80ml marsala
4 teaspoons (14g) dried yeast
180ml warm milk
1 teaspoon caster sugar
375g plain flour
55g caster sugar, extra
1 teaspoon salt
125g butter, chopped finely, softened
1 teaspoon vanilla extract
2 eggs
2 egg yolks
1 egg, beaten lightly, extra

1 Combine fruit and marsala in a small bowl; stand 30 minutes.
2 Whisk yeast, milk and sugar in a small bowl until yeast dissolves. Cover; stand in a warm place about 10 minutes or until frothy.
3 Sift flour, extra sugar and salt into a large bowl; stir in yeast mixture, butter, extract, eggs, egg yolks and undrained fruit mixture. Beat vigorously with a wooden spoon about 5 minutes. (Mixture will be soft like cake batter, but will become elastic and start to leave the side of bowl.) Cover bowl; stand in a warm place about 1 hour or until dough has doubled in size.
4 Grease a deep 20cm round cake tin; line base and side with baking parchment, extending the paper 5cm above sides.
5 Beat dough again with a wooden spoon 5 minutes; spread mixture into tin. Cover; stand in a warm place about 1 hour or until doubled in size.
6 Preheat oven to 200°C/180°C fan-assisted.
7 Brush top of panettone with extra egg. Bake about 1 hour 10 minutes or until panettone sounds hollow when tapped with fingertips. Stand panettone in tin 5 minutes; turn, top-side up, onto a wire rack to cool.

prep + cook time 1 hour 30 minutes (+ standing time)
serves 20
tip Panettone will keep in an airtight container for up to 5 days. Freeze panettone for up to 3 months.

VALENTINE CUPCAKES

125g butter, softened
½ teaspoon vanilla extract
150g caster sugar
2 eggs
185g self-raising flour
80ml milk
pink food colouring
2 tablespoons raspberry jam

decorations
80g icing sugar
350g white ready-to-roll icing
pink food colouring
¼ teaspoon vodka
¼ teaspoon pink petal dust
110g raspberry jam, warmed,
    strained

1 Preheat oven to 180°C/160°C fan-assisted. Line 6-hole large or 12-hole standard muffin pan with paper cases.
2 Beat butter, extract, sugar and eggs in small bowl with electric mixer until light and fluffy. Stir in sifted flour and milk, in two batches.
3 Divide mixture evenly between two bowls. Tint one mixture pink; leave other mixture plain. Drop alternate spoonfuls of the two mixtures into cases.
4 Divide jam among cakes, pull a skewer backwards and forwards through mixtures for a swirling effect; smooth surface.
5 Bake large cakes about 30 minutes, small cakes about 20 minutes. Turn cakes onto wire rack to cool.
6 On surface dusted with sifted icing sugar, knead ready-to-roll icing until smooth. Tint icing with pink colouring; knead into icing only until marbled. Roll out icing to a thickness of 5mm. Cut out rounds large enough to cover tops of cakes.

7 Blend vodka with petal dust. Using a fine paint brush, paint mixture in a heart shape onto icing rounds or paint mixture onto a heart-shaped rubber stamp; press lightly onto icing rounds. Pinch edges of rounds with fingers.
8 Brush tops of cakes with jam; top with stamped rounds.

prep + cook time 55 minutes
makes 6 large or 12 small
tips Petal dust, also called blossom dust and lustre dust, is available from cake decorating suppliers and online.
• Rubber stamps are available from cake decorating shops and online.

HOT CROSS BUNS

4 teaspoons (14g) dried yeast
55g caster sugar
375ml warm milk
600g plain flour
1 teaspoon mixed spice
½ teaspoon ground cinnamon
60g butter
1 egg
120g sultanas

flour paste
75g plain flour
2 teaspoons caster sugar
80ml water, approximately

glaze
1 tablespoon caster sugar
1 teaspoon gelatine
1 tablespoon water

1 Whisk yeast, sugar and milk in a small bowl or jug until yeast dissolves. Cover; stand in a warm place about 10 minutes or until mixture is frothy.

2 Sift flour and spices into a large bowl; rub in butter. Stir in yeast mixture, egg and sultanas; mix to a soft, sticky dough. Cover; stand in a warm place about 45 minutes or until dough has doubled in size.

3 Grease a deep 22cm square cake tin.

4 Knead dough on a floured surface about 5 minutes or until smooth and elastic. Divide dough into 16 pieces; knead into balls. Place balls into tin, cover; stand in a warm place about 10 minutes or until buns have risen two-thirds of the way up the pan.

5 Preheat oven to 220°C/200°C fan-assisted.

6 Make flour paste for crosses; place in a piping bag fitted with a small plain tube. Pipe crosses on buns.

7 Bake buns about 30 minutes or until they sound hollow when tapped. Turn buns, top-side up, onto a wire rack.

8 Make glaze; brush hot glaze on hot buns. Cool.

flour paste
Combine flour and sugar in cup. Gradually blend in enough of the water to form a smooth firm paste.

glaze
Stir ingredients in a small saucepan over heat, without boiling, until sugar and gelatine are dissolved.

prep + cook time 1 hour 35 minutes (+ standing time)
makes 16
tip Buns are best made on the day of serving. Unglazed buns can be frozen for up to 3 months.

EASTER CUPCAKES

125g butter, chopped coarsely
75g white eating chocolate,
  chopped coarsely
220g caster sugar
125ml milk
75g plain flour
75g self-raising flour
1 egg

**whipped white chocolate
  ganache**
125ml double cream
375g white eating chocolate,
  chopped coarsely

decorations
12 mini milk chocolate Easter
  eggs

1 Preheat oven to 170°C/150°C fan-assisted. Line 12-hole (80ml) muffin pan with paper cases.
2 Stir butter, chocolate, sugar and milk in small saucepan over low heat until smooth. Transfer mixture to medium bowl; cool 15 minutes.
3 Whisk sifted flours into chocolate mixture, then whisk in egg. Divide mixture between paper cases.
4 Bake about 30 minutes. Stand cakes in pan 5 minutes before turning, top-side up, onto wire rack to cool.
5 Make whipped white chocolate ganache. Spread cakes with ganache. Position Easter eggs in centre of each cake.

**whipped white chocolate
ganache**
Bring cream to the boil in small saucepan; remove from heat. When bubbles subside, add chocolate; stir until smooth. Transfer mixture to small bowl. Cover; refrigerate 30 minutes. Beat with an electric mixer until light and fluffy.

prep + cook time 55 minutes
(+ refrigeration time)
makes 12

BONFIRE NIGHT PUMPKIN SPICE CAKE

2 eggs
165g brown sugar
60ml maple syrup
160ml vegetable oil
340g pumpkin or butternut
    squash, grated coarsely
60g chopped pecans
250g self-raising flour
½ teaspoon bicarbonate of soda
1 teaspoon ground allspice
2 teaspoons ground cinnamon
1 teaspoon ground ginger
¼ teaspoon ground cinnamon,
    extra

sugared pecans
160g pecan halves
40g icing sugar

maple frosting
375g cream cheese, softened,
    chopped
200g butter, softened
80ml maple syrup
320g icing sugar

1 Preheat oven to 180°C/160°C fan-assisted. Grease a 20cm x 30cm rectangular tin; line base and long sides with baking parchment, extending the paper 5cm over edges.
2 Beat eggs, sugar, syrup and oil in a small bowl with an electric mixer for 5 minutes or until thick and creamy. Transfer mixture to a large bowl; stir in pumpkin and nuts, then sifted dry ingredients. Spread mixture into tin.
3 Bake cake for 30 minutes or until a skewer inserted into the centre comes out clean. Stand cake in tin for 5 minutes before turning, top-side up, onto a wire rack to cool.
4 Meanwhile, make sugared pecans, then maple frosting.
5 Split cake in half. Place the bottom cake layer on a cake plate; spread with half the frosting. Finish with top cake layer and remaining frosting. Decorate with sugared pecans; dust with extra ground cinnamon.

sugared pecans
Rinse nuts in a sieve under cold water until wet. Spread nuts, in a single layer, on a baking-parchment-lined oven tray. Dust with sifted icing sugar. Roast in oven for 10 minutes or until browned lightly.

maple frosting
Beat cream cheese and butter in a small bowl with an electric mixer for 3 minutes or until fluffy and smooth. Gradually beat in syrup and sifted icing sugar until smooth and combined.

prep + cook time 1 hour 40 minutes
serves 12
tip This cake can be made and frosted a day ahead; refrigerate. Stand at room temperature for at least 1 hour before serving. Sugared pecans can be made several days ahead; store in an airtight container at room temperature. Decorate cake with pecans just before serving.

GLOSSARY

allspice also known as pimento or jamaican pepper; so-named because it tastes like a combination of nutmeg, cumin, clove and cinnamon. Available whole (a dark-brown berry the size of a pea) or ground, and used in both sweet and savoury dishes.

baking parchment a silicone-coated paper that is primarily used for lining baking tins and oven trays so cakes and biscuits won't stick, making removal easy.

baking powder raising agent consisting of two parts cream of tartar to one part bicarbonate of soda.

bicarbonate of soda used as a leavening agent in baking.

butter we use salted butter unless stated otherwise. Unsalted or 'sweet' butter has no salt added and is perhaps the most popular butter among pastry-chefs.

buttermilk originally the term given to the slightly sour liquid left after butter was churned from cream, today it is made from skimmed or low-fat milk to which specific bacterial cultures have been added. Despite its name, it is actually low in fat.

chocolate
dark cooking good for cooking as it doesn't require tempering and sets at room temperature. Made with vegetable fat instead of cocoa butter so it lacks the rich, buttery flavour of eating chocolate. Cocoa butter is the most expensive component in chocolate, so the substitution of a vegetable fat means that

compounded chocolate is much cheaper to produce.
dark eating a luxury chocolate made with a high percentage of cocoa liquor and cocoa butter, and little added sugar. Unless otherwise stated, we used dark eating chocolate as it's ideal for use in desserts and cakes.
white contains no cocoa solids but derives its sweet flavour from cocoa butter. Very sensitive to heat so watch carefully when melting.

cinnamon available in pieces (cinnamon sticks) and ground into powder; one of the world's most common spices, used as a sweet, fragrant flavouring for both sweet and savoury foods.

cocoa powder also known as unsweetened cocoa; cocoa beans (cacao seeds) that have been fermented, roasted, shelled, ground into powder then cleared of most of the fat content. Unsweetened cocoa is used in hot chocolate drink mixtures; milk powder and sugar are added to the ground product.

coconut
chips dried, flaked coconut flesh; available raw and toasted.
desiccated dried, unsweetened, finely shredded coconut.
shredded unsweetened thin strips of dried coconut flesh.

condensed milk a canned milk product consisting of milk with more than half the water content removed and sugar added to the milk that remains.

currants dried tiny, almost black raisins so named from the grape

type native to Corinth, Greece; most often used in jams, jellies and sauces.

cornflour also known as cornstarch; used as a thickening agent in cooking.

cream cheese a soft cow's-milk cheese with a fat content ranging from 14 per cent to 33 per cent.

custard powder instant mixture used to make pouring custard.

dates fruit of the date palm tree, eaten fresh or dried. Oval and plump, thin-skinned, with a honey-sweet flavour and sticky texture. Famously found in sticky toffee pudding, as well as in muesli; muffins, scones and cakes; compotes and stewed fruit desserts.

essence/extract an essence is either a distilled concentration of a food quality or an artificial creation of it. Coconut and almond essences are synthetically produced substances used in small amounts to impart their respective flavours to foods. An extract is made by actually extracting the flavour from a food product. In the case of vanilla, pods are soaked, usually in alcohol, to capture the authentic flavour. Essences and extracts keep indefinitely if stored in a cool dark place.

flour
plain unbleached wheat flour, which is the best for baking: the gluten content ensures a strong dough, for a light result.
self-raising plain flour sifted with baking powder (a raising agent consisting mainly of 2 parts cream

of tartar to 1 part bicarbonate of soda) in the proportion of 150g flour to 2 level teaspoons baking powder.

wholemeal also known as wholewheat flour; milled with the wheat germ so is higher in fibre and more nutritional than plain flour.

food colouring vegetable-based substance available in liquid, paste or gel form.

ginger also known as green or root ginger; the thick gnarled root of a tropical plant.

glacé fresh ginger root preserved in sugar syrup.

ground also called powdered ginger; used as a flavouring in baking but cannot be substituted for fresh ginger.

golden syrup a by-product of refined sugarcane; pure maple syrup or honey can be substituted. Treacle is more viscous, and has a stronger flavour and aroma than golden syrup.

maple syrup distilled from the sap of sugar maple trees found only in Canada and the USA. Maple-flavoured syrup or pancake syrup is not an adequate substitute for the real thing.

marsala a fortified Italian wine produced in the region surrounding the Sicilian city of Marsala; recognisable by its intense amber colour and complex aroma. Often used in cooking, especially in sauces, risottos and desserts.

marzipan made from ground almonds, sugar and glucose.

Similar to almond paste but is not as strong in flavour; is finer in consistency and more pliable. Cheaper brands often use ground apricot kernels and sugar.

mascarpone a cultured cream product made in much the same way as yogurt. It's whitish to creamy yellow in colour, with a soft, creamy texture.

mixed spice a classic spice mixture generally containing caraway, allspice, coriander, cumin, nutmeg and ginger, although cinnamon and other spices can be added. It is used with fruit and in cakes.

mixed peel candied citrus peel.

nutmeg a strong and pungent spice ground from the dried nut of an evergreen tree native to Indonesia. Usually found ground but the flavour is more intense from a whole nut, so it's best to grate your own.

orange blossom water concentrated flavouring made from orange blossoms. It is available from the bakery section of most supermarkets.

prunes commercially or sun-dried plums; store in the fridge.

raisins dried sweet grapes (traditionally muscatel grapes).

roasting nuts and dried coconut can be roasted in the oven to restore their fresh flavour and release their aromatic essential oils. Spread them evenly onto a baking tray then roast in a moderate oven for about 5 minutes. Desiccated coconut, pine nuts and sesame seeds roast more evenly if stirred over low

heat in a heavy-based frying pan; their natural oils will help turn them golden brown.

rosewater extract made from crushed rose petals; available from health food stores and good supermarkets.

semolina a hard part of the wheat which is sifted out and used mainly for making pasta.

sugar
brown (light and dark) a very soft, fine sugar retaining molasses for its flavour.
caster finely granulated table sugar.
demerara small-grained golden-coloured crystal sugar.
granulated coarse table sugar, also known as crystal sugar.
icing granulated sugar crushed to a powder; sift well before use.

sultanas dried seedless white grapes.

treacle thick, dark syrup not unlike molasses; a by-product of sugar refining.

vanilla
extract obtained from vanilla pods infused in water.
paste made from vanilla pods and containing real seeds. It is highly concentrated – 1 teaspoon replaces a whole vanilla pod. Found in most supermarkets in the baking section.
pod dried, long, thin pod from a tropical golden orchid; the minuscule black seeds inside the pod impart a luscious flavour in baking and desserts. Place a whole pod in a jar of sugar to make vanilla sugar; a pod can be used three or four times.

INDEX

CONVERSION CHARTS

measures

One metric tablespoon holds 20ml; one metric teaspoon holds 5ml.

All cup and spoon measurements are level. The most accurate way of measuring dry ingredients is to weigh them. When measuring liquids, use a clear glass or plastic jug with metric markings.

We use large eggs with an average weight of 60g.

dry measures

METRIC	IMPERIAL
15g	½oz
30g	1oz
60g	2oz
90g	3oz
125g	4oz (¼lb)
155g	5oz
185g	6oz
220g	7oz
250g	8oz (½lb)
280g	9oz
315g	10oz
345g	11oz
375g	12oz (¾lb)
410g	13oz
440g	14oz
470g	15oz
500g	16oz (1lb)
750g	24oz (1½lb)
1kg	32oz (2lb)

liquid measures

METRIC	IMPERIAL
30ml	1 fluid oz
60ml	2 fluid oz
100ml	3 fluid oz
125ml	4 fluid oz
150ml	5 fluid oz
190ml	6 fluid oz
250ml	8 fluid oz
300ml	10 fluid oz
500ml	16 fluid oz
600ml	20 fluid oz
1000ml (1 litre)	32 fluid oz

length measures

METRIC	IMPERIAL
3mm	⅛in
6mm	¼in
1cm	½in
2cm	¾in
2.5cm	1in
5cm	2in
6cm	2½in
8cm	3in
10cm	4in
13cm	5in
15cm	6in
18cm	7in
20cm	8in
23cm	9in
25cm	10in
28cm	11in
30cm	12in (1ft)

oven temperatures

These are fan-assisted temperatures. If you have a conventional oven (ie. not fan-assisted), increase temperatures by 10–20°.

	°C (CELSIUS)	°F (FAHRENHEIT)	GAS MARK
Very low	100	210	½
Low	130	260	1–2
Moderately low	140	280	3
Moderate	160	325	4–5
Moderately hot	180	350	6
Hot	200	400	7–8
Very hot	220	425	9